SENDING UP MY TIMBER

an african american prayer journal

Eunice,
you are dear to my heart; I
appreciate you for. just
being you — a precious and
mighty woman of God. Continue
to grow in the Lord and trust
Him always. Remember — Prayer is
a powerful weapon against the
devil's dart.

Karen F. Williams *Pray Always*

Lloyd Preston Terrell *Love,*

Introduction by Samuel D. Proctor *Karen F. Wms*
12/31/98

P.S. Praying for you — especially
on May 2 and May 3.

UPPER
ROOM BOOKS
NASHVILLE

Upper Room Web address: http://www.upperroom.org

Scripture quotations designated KJV are from the King James Version of the Bible.

Scripture quotations designated NKJV are from The New King James Version. Copyright © 1979, 1980, 1982, Thomas Nelson Inc., Publishers. Used by permission.

Scripture quotations designated NRSV are from the New Revised Standard Version of the Bible, copyright © 1989 by the Division of Christian Education, National Council of the Churches of Christ in the United States of America. Used by permission.

Scripture quotations designated NIV are from the Holy Bible: New International Version. Copyright © 1973, 1978, 1984 International Bible Society. Used by permission of Zondervan Bible Publishers.

Scripture quotations designated TEV are from Today's English Version—Second Edition © 1992 by American Bible Society.

Excerpt from *From One Brother to Another* is used by permission of Roosevelt Darby, Jr.

Excerpt from "Missing Jonathan" by Renita J. Weems is reprinted by permission of *The Other Side*, 300 W. Apsley St., Philadelphia, PA 19144 (Phone: 215-849-2178).

Excerpt from "Blocking the Prayers of the Church" by Eugene F. Rivers 3d is reprinted with permission from *Sojourners*, 2401 15th St. NW, Washington, DC 20009 (Phone: 202-328-8842 / 800-714-7474).

Excerpt from prayer by Dr. James Forbes, Jr. in *Guide My Feet* by Marian Wright Edelman is used by permission of Dr. Forbes, Senior Minister of The Riverside Church of New York.

Excerpt from "Women of Faith" by Dr. Ella Pearson Mitchell in *No Other Help I Know: Sermons on Prayer and Spirituality* is used by permission of Dr. Mitchell, visiting professor at ITC, Interdenominational Theological Center, Atlanta, Georgia.

Excert from "Prayer Can Be a Real Eye-Opener!" by Dr. Kevin Cosby from *No Other Help I Know: Sermons on Prayer and Spirituality* is used by permission of Dr. Cosby.

Excert from *When Do You Talk to God?* by Patricia C. and Fredrick L. McKissack is used by permission of Patricia C. McKissack.

Excerpt from "A Conversation with Marian Wright Edelman" first published in *Alive Now* (July/August 1997) is used here by permission of Marian Wright Edelman, founder and president of the Children's Defense Fund.

Appreciation is expressed to the Reverend Percell Perkins and Roderick Rogers for sharing with readers from their life experiences.

Cover design: Sheila Williams
Interior design and layout: Sheila Williams and Nancy Cole
First printing: 1998

Library of Congress Cataloging-in-Publication Data
Williams, Karen F., 1959-
 Sending up my timber : an African American prayer journal / Karen F. Williams, Lloyd Preston Terrell.
  p. cm.
 Includes bibliographical references.
 ISBN: 0-8358-0856-4
 1. Afro-Americans—Prayer-books and devotions—English. 2. Devotional calendars. 3. Spiritual journals—Authorship. I. Terrell, Lloyd Preston. II. Title.
 BR563.N4W52   1998   98-6263
 242'.6—dc21   CIP

Printed in the United States of America

Dedication

To my mother, Nettie M. Williams,
who taught me the power and value of prayer
(KFW)

To my dear wife and prayer partner,
Marguerite Carter Terrell,
whose quiet prayer life has made me
a stronger Christian man
(LPT)

Contents

Sending Up My Timber

There's a dream that I dream
Of my heavenly, heavenly home,
And I know that I'm going there one day.
And Oh-Lord—
It may be morning, night or noon,
I don't know just how soon—
That's why I'm sending on up my timber
Every, every, every day.
Oh, yes I am.

Said I'm sending up my timber,
On up to glory,
Every, every day
And oh there's a mansion somewhere in glory
That the Lord has prepared for you and me
And oh-oh—

It may be morning, night or noon
Yes, I don't know, children,
Just how soon.
That's why I'm sending on up my timber
Every, every, every day.

— LLOYD WOODARD

"SENDING UP MY TIMBER" was recorded in 1961 by the Five Blind Boys of Mississippi. This quartet, whose members were all sight-deprived, began in 1939 in Pineywood, Mississippi. According to the Reverend Percell Perkins, organizer and manager of the group (the Five Blind Boys of Mississippi), "Sending Up My Timber" was birthed in 1951 at a sawmill in Mississippi. Perkins relayed that as wood or timber was used to establish and build homes, likewise when we pray we are "sending up timber" to build up our spiritual homes, our faith.

The prayer tradition of contemporary Black worship, like music and preaching, rooted in Africa, has been nurtured in meeting houses and personal prayer lives of slaves and remains a means of vital force for spiritual release and fulfillment. . . . One can "have a little talk with Jesus" and know that everything will be all right.

—MELVA WILSON COSTEN

PAUL'S PITHY EXHORTATION in 1 Thessalonians 5:17, "pray without ceasing" (KJV), has prevailed in the African American experience because "having a little talk with Jesus" has been our livelihood. We knew that if our prayers ceased, then so would we. So we maintained this "vital force for spiritual release" that has enabled us to live in the midst of despair, yet hope for a brighter tomorrow.

Sending Up My Timber is a journal that will enable you to maintain hope and faith by communing with God. The focus of the journal is to encourage you as an individual as well as prayer groups to pray for a specific concern on a daily basis.

This journal contains monthly meditations and Negro spirituals, weekly quotations by a diversity of African Americans, daily scriptures and prayer concerns, and space for journaling, all to provide you with spiritual nourishment as you converse with God. We are also honored to provide an introductory meditation by the late Dr. Samuel D. Proctor to assist you in centering your thoughts on prayer.

It is our hope that as you seek the face of God, you will not only experience God working through you, but you will also see God bringing restoration, healing, salvation, and deliverance to your family, community, city, and the world as promised in 2 Chronicles 7:14 (KJV):

> If my people, which are called by my name, shall humble themselves, and pray, and seek my face, and turn from their wicked ways; then will I hear from heaven, and will forgive their sin, and will heal their land.

A Word of Thanks

We extend words of gratitude to a host of persons who played a vital role in bringing this work into fruition. First, we offer ultimate gratitude to God, who gave us the vision for this journal and the strength to complete it. We are thankful for the following intercessors, journalers, editorial persons who took the time to review this work at various stages and to provide constructive evaluations: John and Gloria Penn, Angela Denmark, Delores Steele, Gwendolyn Colvin, Debora Knowles, Ann Williams, and Mitchell and Marie Johnson. We are thankful for Sheila Williams, who created this book's exquisite cover design. We are also indebted to Bessie McDalton, Doris Bernard, Paul Knox, Charles Courtney, Cleopatra Wingard, Alice Terrell, and Rev. Ruth B. Higgins for their assistance in preparing this manuscript. We deeply appreciate JoAnn Miller for guiding us through the project. Last, we are grateful for the loving support of our families and friends, who prayed for us and encouraged us as we labored diligently to get our words into print.

A Personal Journal

ONE ESSENTIAL PURPOSE of this journal is to provide a place for you to record your prayers, your prayer requests, and your reflections—your talks with God. In *A Thirty-Day Experiment in Prayer* Robert Wood reveals a fitting benefit of a prayer journal:

> A prayer journal provides you an opportunity of gaining new strengths, new insights, and new affirmations of your personal call to be one of Christ's disciples. It is not a secret formula for making you a more mature Christian. But, as in many things, it will become more meaningful to the degree that you put yourself to the task of making sense of God's participation in your life.

Yes, this journal will indeed enable you to see the hand of God gently aiding, directing, and protecting you in your daily walk with him. On some days, however, you may not be compelled to write anything, and that is perfectly all right. Record your entries as you feel led to do so. At another time you might meditate on the scripture for the day and allow God to provide insight and encouragement. God may speak to your heart through a quotation for the week on another day. Just be open to the Holy Spirit's leading in your life. This is your private time with God.

During your prayer time, pray specifically. On June 8, for example, when you are praying for bereaved fathers, pray specifically for persons that you know—in your family, church, community—by calling their names to God. Remember to pray for yourself as well when a particular concern relates to you.

Remember, God's presence and strength abides with you in your personal prayer time, as well as when you pray corporately. Matthew 18:20 confirms, "For where two or three are gathered together in my name, there am I in the midst of them" (KJV). You need God in the midst—in the center of all that you do so that God may order your steps.

Realizing the strength that comes from joining others in prayer, we have listed below ways that prayer groups, families, prayer partners, and other gatherings can use this journal. Do not feel compelled to follow rigidly these group suggestions. They are merely guides or models to aid you in your group. Be open, therefore, and prayerful to the way God may direct your group to use this journal.

Prayer Groups

Intercessory prayer groups will find this journal to be a helpful guide. Prayer leaders can encourage each person to obtain a copy of the journal. The leader should emphasize to members of the group that what they write in their journals is private, and they will not be asked to share any of their entries (unless they desire to do so). The main group use of the journal is to pray for the daily concerns.

When the group meets—usually on a weekly basis—the leader can display that particular week's concerns on a board or sheet and the group can pray together. For example, if the group meets on July 15, they would pray for concerns listed for July 9–15 (teens on drugs, children awaiting adoption, latchkey children, sexually abused children, incarcerated youth, neglected children, and children in custody battles). As stated in the section "A Personal Journal," the group can pray specifically for persons they know who are struggling with the concerns to make the prayer as directed and personal as possible.

The scripture passages can also be used with the group. The leader can set aside a time for members to talk together about how God has spoken to them through one of the scripture passages. If a quotation or meditation has been a source of inspiration, members might talk about this as well.

Family Prayer

Families can use this journal to enhance their prayer life. By setting aside designated times to pray each day for different concerns listed in the journal as well as each member's needs, families will grow closer to God and one another. Discussions can center around the daily scriptures listed as well as the weekly quotations and monthly meditations.

Prayer Partners

If you have a prayer partner, the two of you can pray for each day's particular need. For example, if you pray together on August 6, then you would offer up intercession for "safety for families on vacation." Pray specifically, calling the names of families you know who are traveling. You can also agree to pray for the week's concerns as suggested for prayer groups.

Other Small Groups

Small groups—such as a Bible study, a women's group, a community Bible study—that already have a designated agenda or course outline might use the daily prayer concerns and scriptures in this journal as their focus during the opening and/or closing prayer. The meditations also might be chosen to use as opening devotionals for a small-group session.

Additional Resources

Sending Up My Timber does not teach how to pray, but Upper Room Books has an excellent selection of books that will guide you in this process. Listed below are some of their publications that will enhance your prayer life.

- *Beginning Prayer*
- *The Workbook on Intercessory Prayer*
- *Prayers for Prisoners*
- *Prayers for My Village*
- *My Journal: A Place to Write about God and Me* (A children's journal for ages seven through twelve)
- *Children and Prayer*

MY WORK AS a Christian pastor and teacher of practical theology made it possible for me to meet and know the Reverend Dr. Samuel Dewitt Proctor, Pastor Emeritus of Abyssinian Baptist Church. I consulted with Dr. Proctor on theological issues, the pastorate, preaching, and on the subject of prayer. Proctor was not only a Christian leader, theologian, educator, pastor, and community activist, he was also a man who lived a disciplined devotional life through prayer. He defined prayer as "our dialogue with God." Such a dialogue with God acknowledges the amazing fact that at all times, we can go to God in prayer. Therefore, it seemed appropriate and right for Karen F. Williams and me to ask Dr. Proctor, a man who had influenced thousands of pastors and people about the power of God and prayer, to write the following introduction for *Sending Up My Timber*. His words of insight and spiritual power take on greater significance because they were written several months before his untimely death in May 1997.

— LLOYD PRESTON TERRELL

AUTHOR'S NOTE

PRAYER IS AS IMPORTANT in the life of a Christian as oxygen is to our lungs and as carbon dioxide is to the strength of trees. It is the ingredient without which there is no life. Prayer is more than a shopping list that we present to God, more than a registration of our complaints, more than a recitation of our righteousness, and more than a mild plea for the forgiveness of minimized sins.

God must be amused at some of the pretense and self-deception in our praying. Once a minister asked me if I would invite him to preach at Abyssinian Church. When I explained to him how remote such a possibility it was, he then asked me if he could come and pray! What on earth did he think a prayer was that it required such an audience? And, really, what did he think a minister was?

Despite such misrepresentation of prayer, we follow our Master's example, and we keep open our dialogue with God. We do as Paul admonished, and we "pray without ceasing." Prayer is a unique form of communication, telling God what God always knows, thanking God for grace that we never deserve and asking for what God knows we need and wants to provide for us. It is like being in love and repeating to one another what each one already knows. So prayer is an act of affirmation and concord, consent and commitment, conciliation and trust.

We realize how prayer defies logic, and how it seems to contradict the natural order of things, but we have a native heart-hunger to be in communion with God. As Augustine said, "Our restless souls shall find no rest until they rest in Thee." The psalmist said we "thirst" for the living God.

For all of these centuries prayer has persisted as a faith proposition, and no one had any hard evidence that a busy and majestic Creator had time to hear our mumblings as we knelt beside our beds. We offered our testimonies of answered prayers, but the skeptics were waiting for more evidence.

Today we sit at our fax machines and send messages all over the world. The air is cluttered with unseen conversations from ship to shore, from space capsules to Houston, from laboratories to hospitals, from jet planes to towers. Teenagers play with computers and talk to strangers a long way from home. One wonders how these messages get through with the airwaves so loaded. And if the atmosphere has a secret way of relaying such messages from continent to continent among mere humans, what should be so surprising about a mighty and all-powerful God being in communication with us? God made the airwaves and all that they are capable of doing.

Well, our feeble ways of knowing are fit for humans. These computers tell us that there are other ways of knowing and communicating that have been here all the time, since Abraham came out of Ur of the Chaldees, and we are just finding these avenues of communication. We believe that prayer is one of those ancient, yet abiding, ways available for us to talk with God.

— SAMUEL D. PROCTOR

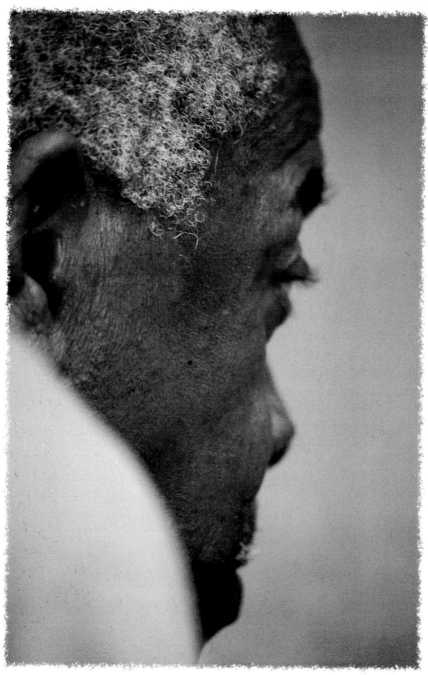

STANDIN' IN THE NEED OF PRAYER

Not my brother, nor my sister, but it's me, O Lord,
Standin' in the need of prayer;
Not my brother, nor my sister, but it's me, O Lord,
Standin' in the need of prayer.

Chorus:
It's me, it's me, it's me, O Lord,
Standin' in the need of prayer;
It's me, it's me, it's me, O Lord,
Standin' in the need of prayer.

Not the preacher, nor the deacon, but it's me, O Lord,
Standin' in the need of prayer.
Not the preacher, nor the deacon, but it's me, O Lord,
Standin' in the need of prayer.

(Repeat Chorus)

Not my father, nor my mother, but it's me, O Lord,
Standin' in the need of prayer.
Not my father, nor my mother, but it's me, O Lord,
Standin' in the need of prayer.

(Repeat Chorus)

Not the stranger, nor my neighbor, but it's me, O Lord,
Standin' in the need of prayer.
Not the stranger, nor my neighbor, but it's me, O Lord,
Standin' in the need of prayer.

(Repeat Chorus)

JANUARY

PRAYERS
FOR THE
SOUL

Knowing the Condition of My Soul

In de Lord, in de Lord, my soul's been anchored in de Lord.

— NEGRO SPIRITUAL

MANY OF US LIVE OUR LIVES never asking, "What is the condition of my soul?" When we have outbursts of uncontrollable anger or keep the extra dollars that the cashier mistakenly gives us, it is a matter of the soul rather than irritation or luck. What is the condition of the soul when we are critical of others and others are critical of us? To discover the state of the soul we must examine our heart to see what is really going on. Is our heart filled with faith and expectancy, or doubt and despondency? When we examine our heart, we allow God to get to the root of why we act the way we do.

Stress from increasing demands or sin that has taken residence in our being has left many souls in a condition of despair and hopelessness. There are people who feel overwhelming pressures from relationships or circumstances. And sin leaves persons drained and powerless because there seems to be no way out. But prayer is a sure way by which we can know the state of our souls and to find hope as we face the living of our days.

In *Meditations of the Heart,* Dr. Howard Thurman writes that "the only possibility of stability for the person, is to establish an Island of Peace within one's soul." Through prayer my soul has experienced peace because I spent time alone with God. Spending time with God in prayer opens the floodgates for the Lord to shower our souls with peace, restoration, and guidance for right living.

Who can escape or be free from the problems and challenges of this present age? Every person must face some kind of trial. Perhaps you have just learned that you have been terminated from your job. Are you the person whose child is on drugs? Do you have a loved one in a gang or cult? Has the doctor told you that you are terminally ill? How have these heartaches determined the condition of your soul? The stresses and disappointments of daily living will shake one's foundation, but the soul that goes to God in prayer will not be shaken.

In Psalm 42:2, the psalmist prayed about the condition of the soul. He said, "My soul thirsts for God, for the living God. When shall I come and appear before God?" (NKJV). As the psalmist hungered to be delivered from his enemies, his soul hungered to know the presence and peace that only God can give.

During the days of slavery, our ancestors' souls also hungered to be delivered from bondage. Their prayers to a living God have taught us much about the condition of the soul, especially as we read and hear the words of this Negro spiritual: "Goin' shout an' pray an' never stop. My soul's been anchored in de Lord." This spiritual teaches us to pray and never stop praying no matter what we face. The slaves were able to endure slavery and maintain hope for freedom because their souls were anchored— connected to God in prayer.

For the next thirty-one days make it a priority to know the condition of your soul. Get alone with God in prayer. Establish a time for peace to be restored in your soul.

PRAYER: O God, restore the souls of your people with the peace of the Holy Spirit. Guide us on the paths of holiness. We give you the glory and honor for every breakthrough. In Jesus' name. Amen.

(LPT)

January 1

PRAYER CONCERN: Finding new ways to show love

By this all will know that you are My disciples, if you have love for one another (John 13:35, NKJV).

January 2

PRAYER CONCERN: Experiencing joy

Nehemiah said, "Go and enjoy choice food and sweet drinks, and send some to those who have nothing prepared. This day is sacred to our Lord. Do not grieve, for the joy of the Lord is your strength" (Neh. 8:10, NIV).

**PRAYER CONCERN: Having peace that
comes from dependence on God**

January
3

Those of steadfast mind you keep in peace—
in peace because they trust in you
(Isa. 26:3, NRSV).

PRAYER CONCERN: Striving to be patient

January
4

Be completely humble and gentle; be
patient, bearing with one another in love
(Eph. 4:2, NIV).

PRAYER CONCERN: Living a life of humility

As God's chosen people, holy and dearly loved, clothe yourselves with compassion, kindness, humility, gentleness and patience (Col. 3:12, NIV).

PRAYER CONCERN: Judging others fairly

Judge not, that ye be not judged (Matt. 7:1, KJV).

PRAYER CONCERN: Handling the area in which I lack self-control

You must make every effort to support your faith with goodness, and goodness with knowledge, and knowledge with self-control, and self-control with endurance, and endurance with godliness (2 Peter 1:5-6, NRSV).

January 7

We can all admit our sinfulness to God; after all, it is no surprise to him; he is already aware of everything we do.

— Marjorie L. Kimbrough

PRAYER CONCERN: Learning to handle anger

Be angry, and do not sin. Meditate within your heart on your bed, and be still (Psalm 4:4, NKJV).

January 8

January
9

PRAYER CONCERN: Having faith and confidence in God's power

Not by might, nor by power, but by my spirit, saith the Lord of hosts (Zech. 4:6*b*, KJV).

January
10

PRAYER CONCERN: Using my gifts for God's glory

As each one has received a gift, minister it to one another, as good stewards of the manifold grace of God (1 Peter 4:10, NKJV).

PRAYER CONCERN: Seeking deliverance from what holds me in bondage

Therefore since we are surrounded by such a great cloud of witnesses, let us throw off everything that hinders and the sin that so easily entangles, and let us run with perseverance the race marked out for us (Heb. 12:1, NIV).

January
11

January
12

PRAYER CONCERN: Hearing God's word and obeying it

Blessed are those who do His commandments, that they may have the right to the tree of life, and may enter through the gates into the city (Rev. 22:14, NKJV).

January
13

PRAYER CONCERN: **Overcoming my fears**
"Do not be afraid . . . for I myself will help you,"
declares the Lord, your Redeemer, the Holy
One of Israel (Isa. 41:14, NIV).

*We often pray for
what we want and
not what we need. . . .
No wonder the saints
of another era coined
the folk-saying on
prayer: "Lord, teach
us to pray and what
to pray for."*
— Wyatt Tee Walker

January
14

PRAYER CONCERN: **Recommitting
my life to God**
Commit thy way unto the Lord; trust also
in him; and he shall bring it to pass
(Psalm 37:5, KJV).

**PRAYER CONCERN: Identifying areas where
I exhibit a proud or arrogant attitude**
Pride goeth before destruction, and an
haughty spirit before a fall (Prov. 16:18, KJV).

January
15

PRAYER CONCERN: Having a discerning spirit
Solomon said, "Give therefore thy servant
an understanding heart to judge thy people,
that I may discern between good and bad"
(1 Kings 3:9, KJV).

January
16

January 17

PRAYER CONCERN: Using God's money responsibly

The wicked borrow and do not repay, but the righteous give generously (Psalm 37:21, NIV).

January 18

PRAYER CONCERN: Desiring a good name

A good name is more desirable than great riches; to be esteemed is better than silver or gold (Prov. 22:1, NIV).

PRAYER CONCERN: Being trustworthy
Many proclaim themselves loyal, but who can find one worthy of trust? (Prov. 20:6, NRSV)

PRAYER CONCERN: Asking God for wisdom
The fear of the Lord is the beginning of wisdom: and the knowledge of the holy is understanding (Prov. 9:10, KJV).

January
21

PRAYER CONCERN: Spending time with God daily

In the morning, rising up a great while before day, [Jesus] went out, and departed into a solitary place, and there prayed (Mark 1:35, KJV).

I need to listen to silence and hear the soul's cries. Burdens are too heavy for weak shoulders to bear alone. There must be time to talk to God undisturbed and to listen.

—Woodie W. White

January
22

PRAYER CONCERN: Forgiving others

For if you forgive men when they sin against you, your heavenly Father will also forgive you (Matt. 6:14, NIV).

PRAYER CONCERN: Desiring to seek God

Seek first the kingdom of God and His righteousness, and all these things shall be added to you (Matt. 6:33, NKJV).

January
23

PRAYER CONCERN: Making time to fast

When you fast, put oil on your head and wash your face, so that it will not be obvious to men that you are fasting, but only to your Father, who is unseen; and your Father, who sees what is done in secret, will reward you (Matt. 6:17-18, NIV).

January
24

January 25

PRAYER CONCERN: Being honest and fair

The night is far spent, the day is at hand: let us therefore cast off the works of darkness, and let us put on the armour of light. Let us walk honestly, as in the day (Rom. 13:12-13, KJV).

January 26

PRAYER CONCERN: Doing what God requires

He has told you, O mortal, what is good; and what does the Lord require of you but to do justice, and to love kindness, and to walk humbly with your God? (Micah 6:8, NRSV)

PRAYER CONCERN: Confessing my sin

If we confess our sins, he is faithful and just to forgive us our sins and to cleanse us from all unrighteousness (1 John 1:9, NKJV).

January
27

Lord, before whose eyes the depth of the human conscience is laid bare, what in me could be hidden although I were unwilling to confess it to you? . . . Whatever I am, therefore, O Lord, is laid bare before you.

— African Bishop Augustine of Hippo

PRAYER CONCERN: Having godly motives

Do nothing out of selfish ambition or vain conceit, but in humility consider others better than yourselves (Phil. 2:3, NIV).

January
28

January 29

PRAYER CONCERN: Knowing the condition of my soul

What good will it be for a man if he gains the whole world, yet forfeits his soul? Or what can a man give in exchange for his soul? (Matt. 16:26, NIV)

January 30

PRAYER CONCERN: Trusting in God's word

I shall have an answer for those who taunt me, for I trust in your word (Psalm 119:42, NRSV).

PRAYER CONCERN: Cleansing my heart

Create in me a clean heart, O God; and renew a right spirit within me (Psalm 51:10, KJV).

January

31

CERTAINLY, LORD

Have you got good religion?
Cert'nly, Lord!
Have you got good religion?
Cert'nly, Lord!
Have you got good religion?
Cert'nly, Lord!
Cert'nly, cert'nly, cert'nly, Lord!

Have you been redeemed?
Cert'nly, Lord!
Have you been redeemed?
Cert'nly, Lord!
Have you been redeemed?
Cert'nly, Lord!
Cert'nly, cert'nly, cert'nly, Lord!

Have you been to the water?
Cert'nly, Lord!
Have you been to the water?
Cert'nly, Lord!
Have you been to the water?
Cert'nly, Lord!
Cert'nly, cert'nly, cert'nly, Lord!

Have you been baptized?
Cert'nly, Lord!
Have you been baptized?
Cert'nly, Lord!
Have you been baptized?
Cert'nly, Lord!
Cert'nly, cert'nly, cert'nly, Lord!

FEBRUARY

PRAYERS
FOR THE
CHURCH

Seeking a Vision through Prayer

We asked the church to go on its knees
when doors were closed against us and
everytime we prayed the doors were opened.
— A. CLAYTON POWELL, SR.

OUR CHURCH STRUGGLED for a vision in ministry. We struggled because we placed our attention on programs rather than prayer. We had strategies and master plans from various workshops, but these methods were not working for us. We were so desperate for a vision that we spent more hours seeking advice from the fastest-growing churches in our community than we spent asking God to reveal the vision for our ministry.

Failing in ministry forced me as a pastor to turn to God in prayer. I simply asked God to make the vision for our church known. This vision began to unfold the moment I prayed.

God revealed to us in a planning meeting that we prayed only during worship and before group meetings. An older man who attended the meeting said, "Pastor, I want to ask you a question. How can we have a vision from God for the church when we don't talk to him?" This man's comments made me think of the spiritual, "I Couldn't Hear Nobody Pray":

Lord, I couldn't hear nobody pray
O Lord, I couldn't hear nobody pray,
Oh, way down yonder by myself,
And I couldn't hear nobody pray.

God could not give us a vision because he couldn't hear our church praying.

We then agreed to commit ourselves not only to pray but also to study prayer in order to know how to talk to God and to receive the vision that only God could reveal to us. We organized a School of Prayer composed of thirteen persons. As a result of the school, twelve persons are now leading prayer classes that are dedicated to praying for our church's vision as well as other concerns.

Prayer has changed our church. We have a vision for ministry. In Jeremiah 33:3 the Lord says, "Call to me and I will answer you and tell you great and unsearchable things you do not know" (NIV). This scripture informs us that if we pray, God will tell us what we need to know. We now have spirit-filled worship and unity as a body of Christ. God has given us "great and unsearchable things." Through prayer our church is taking action for ministry in the Black community by establishing an evangelism team, an after-school program, a credit union, and by providing counseling for the family.

God has revealed to us that a church's vision is more than the nuts and bolts of church administration. The vision is more than breaking church-growth records. The vision is about loving and serving God, reaching out through evangelism, and praying for God's will to be done.

We are now certain that the first step in a vision for the church is for the pastor and congregation to pray.

PRAYER: O God, our Teacher, I thank you for your Church. I open my heart to become a praying member so that my local church may truly be a house of prayer. Teach me how to be constant in prayer. In Jesus' name I pray. Amen.

(LPT)

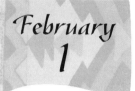

February 1

PRAYER CONCERN: **Those who preach the gospel**

How shall they preach, except they be sent? as it is written, How beautiful are the feet of them that preach the gospel of peace, and bring glad tidings of good things! (Rom. 10:15, KJV)

February 2

PRAYER CONCERN: **Spirit-filled worship**

God is a Spirit: and they that worship him must worship him in spirit and in truth (John 4:24, KJV).

PRAYER CONCERN: Hospitality in the body of Christ

Share with God's people who are in need. Practice hospitality (Rom. 12:13, NIV).

February
3

PRAYER CONCERN: Unity in the body of Christ

If you have any encouragement from being united with Christ, if any comfort from his love, if any fellowship with the Spirit, if any tenderness and compassion, then make my joy complete by being like-minded, having the same love, being one in spirit and purpose (Phil. 2:1-2, NIV).

February
4

February 5

PRAYER CONCERN: Anointed church conferences and conventions

And when they had prayed, the place where they were assembled together was shaken; and they were all filled with the Holy Spirit, and they spoke the word of God with boldness (Acts 4:31, NKJV).

February 6

PRAYER CONCERN: First-time pastors

Be strong in the grace that is in Christ Jesus (2 Tim. 2:1*b*, NIV).

PRAYER CONCERN: The moving of the Holy Spirit in the body of Christ

But you will receive power when the Holy Spirit has come upon you; and you will be my witnesses in Jerusalem, and in all Judea and Samaria, and to the ends of the earth (Acts 1:8, NRSV).

February

7

The habit of praying only when we are in turmoil boxes God into one role in our lives.

— Sheron C. Patterson

PRAYER CONCERN: Gifted teachers to proclaim God's word

The gifts he gave were that some would be apostles, some prophets, some evangelists, some pastors and teachers, to equip the saints for the work of ministry, for building up the body of Christ (Eph. 4:11, NRSV).

February

8

February 9

PRAYER CONCERN: **Anointed pastors**
And I will give you shepherds according to My heart, who will feed you with knowledge and understanding (Jer. 3:15, NKJV).

February 10

PRAYER CONCERN: **Families of pastors**
May the God who gives endurance and encouragement give you a spirit of unity among yourselves as you follow Christ Jesus (Rom. 15:5, NIV).

PRAYER CONCERN: The pastor's staff

The body is a unit, though it is made up of
many parts; and though all its parts are many,
they form one body. So it is with Christ
(1 Cor. 12:12, NIV).

February
11

PRAYER CONCERN: Prayer partners

Again, I say to you that if two of you agree
on earth concerning anything that they ask,
it will done for them by My Father in heaven
(Matt. 18:19, NKJV).

February
12

February
13

PRAYER CONCERN: Effective small-group and cell ministries

And let us consider one another to provoke unto love and to good works: not forsaking the assembling of ourselves together . . . but exhorting one another: and so much the more, as ye see the day approaching (Heb. 10:24-25, KJV).

I believe it is my greatest honor and happiness to be thy disciple; how miserable and blind are those that live without God in the world, who despise the light of Thy holy faith.
— Richard Allen

February
14

PRAYER CONCERN: The ministry of discipleship

If You abide in My word, you are My disciples indeed. And you shall know the truth, and the truth shall make you free (John 8:31*b*-32, NKJV).

PRAYER CONCERN: Those who are to be baptized

For John truly baptized with water; but ye shall be baptized with the Holy Ghost not many days hence (Acts 1:5, KJV).

February **15**

PRAYER CONCERN: Remembering the true purpose of Holy Communion

When [Jesus] had given thanks, He broke [bread] and said, "Take eat; this is My body which is broken for you; do this in remembrance of Me." In the same manner He also took the cup after supper, saying, "This cup is the new covenant in My blood. This do, as often as you drink it, in remembrance of Me" (1 Cor. 11:24-25, NKJV).

February **16**

February 17

PRAYER CONCERN: Those on the mission field

Therefore they that were scattered abroad went every where preaching the word (Acts 8:4, KJV).

February 18

PRAYER CONCERN: Sincere fellowship among believers

[The believers] broke bread in their homes and ate together with glad and sincere hearts, praising God and enjoying the favor of all the people. And the Lord added to their number daily those who were being saved (Acts 2:46b-47, NIV).

PRAYER CONCERN: New Christians

Be imitators of God as dear children
(Eph. 5:1, NKJV).

February
19

**PRAYER CONCERN: Greater servantship
in the church**

Instead the greatest among you should be like
the youngest, and the one who rules like the
one who serves (Luke 22:26*b*, NIV).

February
20

February 21

PRAYER CONCERN: **Those who will be ordained**

Ye have not chosen me, but I have chosen you, and ordained you, that ye should go and bring forth fruit, and that your fruit should remain: that whatsoever ye shall ask of the Father in my name, he may give it you (John 15:16, KJV).

Black Christians often state that "prayer changes things." Prayer frequently changes the conditions and circumstances of our lives. But prayer also changes people—most especially the kingdom-bearers, the change agents of God.

— Preston Robert Washington

February 22

PRAYER CONCERN: **Effective evangelism**

Daily in the temple, and in every house, they did not cease teaching and preaching Jesus as the Christ (Acts 5:42, NKJV).

PRAYER CONCERN: Church revival

Will you not revive us again, that your people
may rejoice in you? (Psalm 85:6, NIV)

February
23

**PRAYER CONCERN: Those persecuted
for the gospel's sake**

And now, Lord, look at their threats, and grant
to your servants to speak your word with all
boldness, while you stretch out your hand to
heal, and signs and wonders are performed
through the name of your holy servant Jesus
(Acts 4:29-30, NRSV).

February
24

February 25

PRAYER CONCERN: All lay ministries

For this reason, since the day we heard about you, we have not stopped praying for you and asking God to fill you with the knowledge of his will through all spiritual wisdom and understanding (Col. 1:9, NIV).

February 26

PRAYER CONCERN: To fulfill the mission of the church

As you go, preach this message: "The Kingdom of heaven is near." Heal the sick, raise the dead, cleanse those who have leprosy, drive out demons. Freely you have received, freely give (Matt. 10:7-8, NIV).

PRAYER CONCERN: To obey God's word

But be doers of the word, and not hearers only, deceiving yourselves (James 1:22, NKJV).

February
27

Prayer, diligence, and effort go together. There is a time to pray, and then a time to act, to move. God seemed to say, "You have prayed—now obey orders."

— Charles T. Walker

PRAYER CONCERN: Church order

All things should be done decently and in order (1 Cor. 14:40, NRSV).

February
28

February 29

PRAYER CONCERN: **The ministry of prayer**

And all things, whatever you ask in prayer, believing, you will receive (Matt. 21:22, NKJV).

© Jeffrey High/IMAGEProductions

EV'RY TIME I FEEL THE SPIRIT

Ev'ry time I feel the Spirit moving in my heart,
I will pray.

Upon the mountain my Lord spoke,
Out His mouth came fire and smoke.
All around me looks so shine,
Ask my Lord if all was mine.

Ev'ry time I feel the Spirit moving in my heart,
I will pray.

Jordan river is chilly and cold,
Chills the body but not the soul.
Ain't but one train on dis track,
Runs to heaven and right back.

Ev'ry time I feel the Spirit moving in my heart,
I will pray.

MARCH

PRAYERS
FOR THE
NATION

Seeking Peace for Our Nation

Prayer equips us for action. Many of us tend to eagerly run out to take on the world's needs without first consulting with the One who can meet those needs.

— JOHN PERKINS

EVERY DAY SOMEONE is praying for national concerns, especially the concerns and issues that creep into the Black community. Individuals and prayer groups are diligent as they pray to bring about changes in the city. Christians pray because we truly believe only God has the power to make the difference so that people can live in our nation's cities free from poverty, violence, crime, and hate. Prayer keeps us imagining the best in humankind.

One of the Bible's most valued scriptures on praying for the city and nation is found in Jeremiah 29:7: "And seek the peace of the city where I have caused you to be carried away captive, and pray to the Lord for it; for in its peace you will have peace" (NKJV). The prophet Jeremiah gives prayerful advice to the Jewish exiles in Babylon to pursue the city's welfare and to pray on the city's behalf. Certainly the Jews wanted to return to Jerusalem, but reality meant that they were to find innovative ways to live wholistic lives in the city of their oppressors.

Black Americans can identify with the longing of the heart to return to their native communities and cities— even to Mother Africa. These former communities are often places where loved ones have nurtured one another. However, the prophets from church pulpits and among community leaders encourage us to continue to seek the welfare of the city through prayer. The streets of the big cities are not as friendly as they were made to believe.

Dr. Martin L. King, Jr. taught us much about praying for the welfare and peace of our cities and nation. During the Civil Rights movement, he taught marchers to pray, even when dogs and water hoses were turned on them. Prayer sustained the marchers and changed our nation.

Although businesses, corporations, and the rich often abandon the cities, God has not turned against the people who are often captive there. Praying folk are convinced that God loves the people in the city, is concerned about them, and invites us to pray for power and guidance to carry out nonviolent Christian social change.

Jeremiah's advice for the exiled Jews to pray on Babylon's behalf gives Black Christians a fresh vision on why we must pray for the city. We pray for the city because, as we pray for the good or betterment of where we live, we will experience God working on behalf of the city.

During the month of March, we are invited to pray for the welfare of our nation. By doing so, we too will be praying for the homeless to be housed, for crime to cease, for prison reform, and for quality education, among other concerns. As we pray, we can be assured that, as John Perkins stated, our prayers are equipping us for action because we are consulting God, who is capable of meeting every need.

PRAYER: Lord God, bless our nation with every good thing from you. Open the doors of justice, equality, and righteousness to everyone. May our streets become safe and pleasant. Empower the church to be your change agent for hope and renewal. We offer this prayer in the name of Jesus, our Prince of Peace. Amen.

(LPT)

March 1

PRAYER CONCERN: Justice for all people

Good will come to him who is generous and lends freely, who conducts his affairs with justice (Psalm 112:5, NIV).

March 2

PRAYER CONCERN: Fairness in our judicial system

Judge not according to the appearance, but judge righteous judgment (John 7:24, KJV).

Therefore all things whatsoever ye would that men should do to you, do ye even so to them: for this is the law and the prophets (Matt. 7:12, KJV).

There was a certain man in Caesarea called Cornelius, a centurion of what was called the Italian Regiment, a devout man and one who feared God with all his household, who gave alms generously to the people, and prayed to God always (Acts 10:1-2, NKJV).

March 5

PRAYER CONCERN: Those who work in public safety

The fear of man brings a snare, but whoever trusts in the Lord shall be safe (Prov. 29:25, NKJV).

March 6

PRAYER CONCERN: A society free of racism

Then Peter opened his mouth and said, "In truth I perceive that God shows no partiality" (Acts 10:34, NKJV).

PRAYER CONCERN: Leaders of the nation

Remind them to be subject to rulers and authorities, to obey, to be ready for every good work (Titus 3:1, NKJV).

March

7

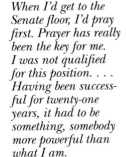

When I'd get to the Senate floor, I'd pray first. Prayer has really been the key for me. I was not qualified for this position. . . . Having been success-ful for twenty-one years, it had to be something, somebody more powerful than what I am.

— Georgia Montgomery Davis Powers

PRAYER CONCERN: Persons who give volunteer service

For we are his workmanship, created in Christ Jesus unto good works, which God hath before ordained that we should walk in them (Eph. 2:10, KJV).

March

8

March 9

PRAYER CONCERN: **The homeless**
The righteous care about justice for the poor,
but the wicked have no such concern
(Prov. 29:7, NIV).

March 10

PRAYER CONCERN: **Victims of crime**
Do not be afraid, for I am with you
(Isa. 43:5, NIV).

PRAYER CONCERN: Feeding the hungry

They also will answer, "Lord, when did we see you hungry or thirsty or a stranger or needing clothes or sick or in prison, and not help you?" He will reply, "I tell you the truth, whatever you did not do for one of the least of these, you did not do for me" (Matt. 25:44-45, NIV).

March **11**

PRAYER CONCERN: Victims of rape

Hear my cry, O God; attend unto my prayer. From the end of the earth will I cry unto thee, when my heart is overwhelmed: lead me to the rock that is higher than I (Psalm 61:1-2, KJV).

March **12**

March 13

PRAYER CONCERN: The oppressed

Then we cried to the Lord, the God of our ancestors; the Lord heard our voice, and saw our affliction, our toil, and our oppression (Deut. 26:7, NRSV).

One night I was so desperate for help that I called on God to free me from the horror of my drug addiction. I began to read the Bible and rely on God's saving grace to get me through my addiction and homelessness.

— Roosevelt Darby Jr.

March 14

PRAYER CONCERN: War on drugs

Paul said, "I appeal to you therefore, brothers and sisters, by the mercies of God, to present your bodies as a living sacrifice, holy and acceptable to God, which is your spiritual worship" (Rom. 12:1, NRSV).

Even the sparrow finds a home, and the swallow a nest for herself, where she may lay her young, at your altars, O Lord of hosts, my King and my God (Psalm 84:3, NRSV).

March
15

Thou shalt not hate thy brother in thine heart: thou shalt in any wise rebuke thy neighbour, and not suffer sin upon him. Thou shall not avenge, nor bear any grudge against the children of thy people, but thou shalt love thy neighbour as thyself: I am the Lord (Lev. 19:17-18, KJV).

March
16

March 17

PRAYER CONCERN: Stewards of the earth

And God said, Let us make man in our image, after our likeness: and let them have dominion over the fish of the sea, and over the fowl of the air, and over the cattle, and over all the earth, and over every creeping thing that creepeth upon the earth (Gen. 1:26, KJV).

March 18

PRAYER CONCERN: Those who practice sexism

But now that faith has come, we are no longer subject to a disciplinarian, for in Christ Jesus you are all children of God through faith. As many of you as were baptized into Christ have clothed yourselves with Christ. There is no longer Jew or Greek, there is no longer slave or free, there is no longer male and female; for all of you are one in Christ Jesus (Gal. 3:25-28, NRSV).

PRAYER CONCERN: For children's defense

For I am the Lord, your God, who takes hold
of your right hand and says to you, Do not fear;
I will help you (Isa. 41:13, NIV).

March
19

**PRAYER CONCERN: Persons who suffer
age discrimination**

Is not wisdom found among the aged? Does not
long life bring understanding? (Job 12:12, NIV)

March
20

March 21

PRAYER CONCERN: Racial reconciliation

Those who say, "I love God," and hate their brothers or sisters, are liars; for those who do not love a brother or sister whom they have seen, cannot love God whom they have not seen (1 John 4:20, NRSV).

A deep level of intercessory prayer will be required to confront the idolatry of white supremacy. It is violent and it can only be dealt with in the most discerning way.

— Eugene F. Rivers 3d

March 22

PRAYER CONCERN: Rights of the physically challenged

For [the Lord] has not despised or disdained the suffering of the afflicted one; he has not hidden his face from him but has listened to his cry for help (Psalm 22:24, NIV).

**PRAYER CONCERN: For the unemployed
to find work**

The Lord is a stronghold for the oppressed,
a stronghold in times of trouble
(Psalm 9:9, NRSV).

March
23

PRAYER CONCERN: Those who clean the city

Whatever you do, work at it with all your heart,
as working for the Lord, not for men, since you
know that you will receive an inheritance from
the Lord as a reward (Col. 3:23-24*a*, NIV).

March
24

March
25

PRAYER CONCERN: Prison reform

Remember those in prison as if you were their fellow prisoners, and those who are mistreated as if you yourselves were suffering (Heb. 13:3, NIV).

March
26

PRAYER CONCERN: Those who live in unsuitable dwellings

I have indeed seen the oppression of my people in Egypt. I have heard their groaning and have come down to set them free (Acts 7:34, NIV).

**PRAYER CONCERN: Restoring and
rebuilding the city**

Then [Nehemiah] said to them, "You see the
trouble we are in, how Jerusalem lies in ruins
with its gates burned. Come, let us rebuild
the wall of Jerusalem, so that we may no longer
suffer disgrace" (Neh. 2:17, NRSV).

*March
27*

*You can make a
difference by praying.
The most important
thing you can do
about any problem
is pray. Pray for
guidance, for
understanding, for
wisdom, for a heart
moved to action.*

— Anthony T.
Evans

**PRAYER CONCERN: Leaders in the
African American community**

May He send you help from the sanctuary,
and strengthen you out of Zion
(Psalm 20:2, NKJV).

*March
28*

March 29

PRAYER CONCERN: Classism

For there is no difference between Jew and Gentile—the same Lord is Lord of all (Rom. 10:12*a*, NIV).

March 30

PRAYER CONCERN: The nation

Righteousness exalts a nation, but sin is a disgrace to any people (Prov. 14:34, NIV).

March 31

PRAYER CONCERN: **Reclaiming the city**

And seek the peace of the city where I have caused you to be carried away captive, and pray to the Lord for it; for in its peace you will have peace (Jer. 29:7, NKJV).

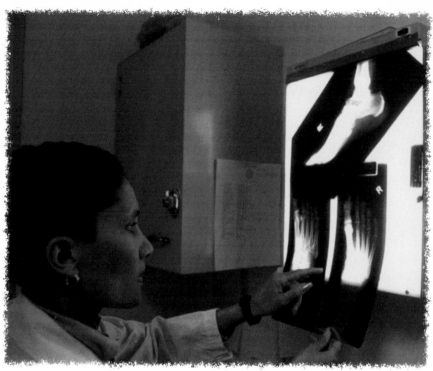

Owen Franken/Corbis

BALM IN GILEAD

There is a balm in Gilead,
to make the wounded whole,
There is a balm in Gilead,
to heal the sin-sick soul.

Sometimes I feel discouraged,
And think my work's in vain,
But then the Holy Spirit
Revives my soul again.

There is a balm in Gilead,
to make the wounded whole,
There is a balm in Gilead,
to heal the sin-sick soul.

Don't ever feel discouraged,
For Jesus is your friend,
And if you look for knowledge,
He'll ne'er refuse to lend.

There is a balm in Gilead,
to make the wounded whole,
There is a balm in Gilead,
to heal the sin-sick soul.

If you cannot preach like Peter,
If you cannot pray like Paul,
You can tell the love of Jesus,
And say "He died for all."

There is a balm in Gilead,
to make the wounded whole,
There is a balm in Gilead,
to heal the sin-sick soul.

PRAYERS
FOR
HEALTH
ISSUES

Partnering with God in Healing

There is a balm in Gilead,
to make the wounded whole,
There is a balm in Gilead,
to heal the sin-sick soul.

WE AS CHRISTIANS have the privileged opportunity to be partners with God in the ministry of healing. In Luke 10:9, Jesus empowered seventy disciples to be in partnership with him to heal the sick and preach the kingdom of God.

God has also invited the medical community to be in partnership with him for healing. Traditional medicine is now linked with complementary medicine. Complementary medicine combines prayer and traditional medical practices. Through research and faith in God, medical experts are discovering something that Christians have known for centuries—there is healing power in prayer. Many years ago, I experienced a person in the medical profession joining me in prayer for my son's healing.

In the summer of 1987, our son Lloyd Jr. was hit in the head with a baseball. He was hospitalized with a fractured skull. Some doctors believed he would have seizures for the remainder of his life, but Lloyd refused to believe what the doctors were saying. Lying in his bed in the intensive care unit, Lloyd said to me, "Father, I'm not going to have seizures; I'm going to be fine."

Later that afternoon, I returned to my church. The phone rang. Dr. Charles Carson was on the line. He was seeking information about the church's health fair. As we talked, I learned that he was a deacon in a church in my community. I told him about Lloyd Jr., and he agreed to meet me in the hospital that evening. Dr. Carson and I

80

knelt at Lloyd's bed and prayed for God to heal him. As partners in prayer, we combined prayer with traditional medicine. In Jeremiah 8:22 the prophet asks, "Is there no balm in Gilead, Is there no physician there?" (NKJV). Our faith in God's healing power promised us that "there is a balm in Gilead to make the wounded whole, there is a balm in Gilead, to heal the sin-sick soul."

My wife taught our son a prayer. Every morning I heard an eleven-year-old boy pray, "Lord, I want my head to be healed. I praise you and believe in your power." James 5:15 tells us that the "prayer of faith will save the sick, and the Lord will raise him up" (NKJV). The Lord healed our son. He was taken off the medicine. He is living a sound, healthy life—and he still plays baseball and basketball!

Although we experienced healing, we as partners with God know that everyone does not always get healed physically. God also heals in spiritual ways. Persons who experience peace about health issues, for example, are often given the faith and power—even in the midst of their pain—to encourage others and offer them hope.

As a pastor, I have learned through visitations with dying parishioners the meaning of spiritual healing. These persons taught me that like Jesus in the Garden of Gethsemane (Mark 14:35-42), their time of pain and suffering did not go away. But faith in Christ gave them hope. Looking to the cross gave these persons healing by way of peace because they trusted God completely.

The partnership that Christians have with God in the ministry of healing opens the way for us to know and accept God's will for our lives. And realizing that we have the compassionate companionship of Almighty God gives us peace and hope.

PRAYER: Living God, we pray for your healing power to be poured on the sick in mind and body. Bless and strengthen those who are afflicted. We claim health and healing in the name of Jesus. Amen.
(LPT)

PRAYER CONCERN: Persons who are HIV-positive or have AIDS

And Jesus went about all the cities and villages, teaching in their synagogues, and preaching the gospel of the kingdom, and healing every sickness and disease among the people (Matt. 9:35, KJV).

PRAYER CONCERN: Hospital and medical center staff

God is not unjust; he will not forget your work and the love you have shown him as you have helped his people and continue to help them (Heb. 6:10, NIV).

**PRAYER CONCERN: Persons with
sickle-cell anemia**

He sent His word and healed them
(Psalm 107:20, NKJV).

PRAYER CONCERN: Persons with hypertension

Casting all your care upon Him, for He cares
for you (1 Pet. 5:7, NJKV).

PRAYER CONCERN: Hospice workers

Jesus said, "But you are those who have continued with Me in My trials" (Luke 22:28, NKJV).

PRAYER CONCERN: Persons with mental disorders

For God hath not given us the spirit of fear; but of power, and of love, and of a sound mind (2 Tim. 1:7, KJV).

PRAYER CONCERN: Healing ministries

[Jesus] called his twelve disciples to him and gave them authority to drive out evil spirits and to cure every kind of disease and sickness (Matt. 10:1, NIV).

Healing is God's work. There is no healing without God. Through prayer we can come into intimate contact with God, the source of all healing, bringing our lives into line with God's healing activity.

— Edward P. Wimberly

PRAYER CONCERN: Persons with fibroid tumors

Then [Jesus] put his hands on her, and immediately she straightened up and praised God (Luke 13:13, NIV).

PRAYER CONCERN: Persons with terminal illnesses

Blessed be the God and Father of our Lord Jesus Christ, the Father of mercies and God of all consolation (2 Cor. 1:3, NRSV).

PRAYER CONCERN: Persons to anoint and pray for the sick

Is anyone among you sick? Let him call for the elders of the church, and let them pray over him, anointing him with oil in the name of the Lord (James 5:14, NKJV).

PRAYER CONCERN: Persons with cancer

Heal me, O Lord, and I shall be healed: save me, and I shall be saved: for thou art my praise (Jer. 17:14, KJV).

PRAYER CONCERN: A spirit of compassion among medical staff

But we were gentle among you, even as a nurse cherisheth her children (1 Thess. 2:7, KJV).

April
13

PRAYER CONCERN: Persons with eye diseases
Then he touched their eyes and said,
"According to your faith will it be done to you";
and their sight was restored (Matt. 9:29, NIV).

*I experienced a
massive heart attack
at the age of nineteen.
While I was being
hospitalized my
condition grew worse
and it seemed as if
I wasn't going to make
it. The church, family,
and friends said many
prayers for me. But
when I, myself, gave
myself to the Lord and
prayed for Him to save
my life, He answered
my prayers and spared
me from my sickness
and pain.*

— Roderick Rogers
(Heart transplant
recipient)

April
14

PRAYER CONCERN: Persons with heart disease
And Jesus went forth, and saw a great multitude,
and was moved with compassion toward them,
and he healed their sick (Matt. 14:14, KJV).

PRAYER CONCERN: Persons recovering after surgery

April 15

Then shall thy light break forth as the morning, and thine health shall spring forth speedily; and thy righteousness shall go before thee; the glory of the Lord shall be thy reward (Isa. 58:8, KJV).

PRAYER CONCERN: Persons with skin disorders

April 16

For I will restore health to you, and your wounds I will heal, says the Lord (Jer. 30:17a, NRSV).

PRAYER CONCERN: Persons with tuberculosis
O Lord my God, I cried unto thee, and thou
hast healed me (Psalm 30:2, KJV).

PRAYER CONCERN: Persons with diabetes
But when the multitudes knew it, they followed
[Jesus]; and He received them and spoke to
them about the kingdom of God, and
healed those who had need of healing
(Luke 9:11, NKJV).

**PRAYER CONCERN: Persons with
nervous disorders**

Do not be anxious about anything, but in everything, by prayer and petition, with thanksgiving, present your requests to God (Phil. 4:6, NIV).

**PRAYER CONCERN: Persons who are
to have surgery**

Let him trust in the name of the Lord and rely upon his God (Isa. 50:10c, NKJV).

PRAYER CONCERN: Those who care for the sick

Therefore encourage one another and
build up each other, as indeed you are doing
(1 Thess. 5:11, NRSV).

*I went in the
bathroom, closed
the do' after I got
her comfortable, and
I talked to God. . . .
Nobody had told me
what to do until I
went in there. Got on
my knees and consult
God and I come outa
there knowin what to
do cause He just
guided my hands.*

— Onnie Lee Logan
(midwife in the
1930s)

**PRAYER CONCERN: Persons with
Alzheimer's disease**

Help me, O Lord my God! Oh, save me
according to Your mercy (Psalm 109:26, NKJV).

PRAYER CONCERN: Those who care for the sick on the Sabbath

Then said Jesus unto them, I will ask you one thing; Is it lawful on the sabbath days to do good, or to do evil? to save life, or to destroy it? (Luke 6:9, KJV)

April 23

PRAYER CONCERN: Better health care for African Americans

I was the eyes to the blind, and I was feet to the lame. I was a father to the poor, and I searched out the case that I did not know (Job 29:15-16, NKJV).

April 24

PRAYER CONCERN: Persons who are facing death

Even though I walk through the darkest valley, I fear no evil; for you are with me; your rod and your staff—they comfort me (Psalm 23:4, NRSV).

PRAYER CONCERN: Victims of medical malpractice

Look upon my affliction and my distress. . . . Guard my life and rescue me; let me not be put to shame, for I take refuge in you (Psalm 25:18, 20, NIV).

PRAYER CONCERN: Good health for persons getting physical examinations

Dear friend, I pray that you may enjoy good health and that all may go well with you, even as your soul is getting along well (3 John 2, NIV).

April
27

I was crippled. I had a hurting in my leg, and I couldn't walk without a stick. Finally, one day I went to go out and pick some turnips. . . . My leg hurt so bad that I talked to the Lord about it. And it seemed to me, He said, "Put down your stick." I put it down, and I ain't used it since.

— Orleans Finger

PRAYER CONCERN: Those who visit the sick and shut-in

I was sick and ye visited me (Matt. 25:36*b*, KJV).

April
28

PRAYER CONCERN: Persons facing a difficult medical decision

[The Lord] restores my soul. He guides me in paths of righteousness for his name's sake (Psalm 23:3, NIV).

PRAYER CONCERN: Those with addictions

God is our refuge and strength, a very present help in trouble (Psalm 46:1, KJV).

STEAL AWAY

Chorus:
Steal away, steal away, steal away to Jesus!
Steal away, steal away home,
I ain't got long to stay here!

My Lord calls me,
He calls me by the thunder;
The trumpet sounds with-in-a my soul,
I ain't got long to stay here.

(Repeat Chorus)

Green trees are bending,
Poor sinner stands a-trembling;
The trumpet sounds with-in-a my soul,
I ain't got long to stay here.

(Repeat Chorus)

Tombstones are bursting,
Poor sinner stands a-trembling;
The trumpet sounds with-in-a my soul,
I ain't got long to stay here.

(Repeat Chorus)

My Lord calls me,
He calls me by the lightning,
The trumpet sounds with-in-a my soul,
I ain't got long to stay here.

MAY

PRAYERS
FOR
WOMEN

Praying in Secret

Steal away, steal away, steal away to Jesus!

THERE WAS NO SYNAGOGUE in Philippi, a Roman colony, since persons were prohibited from bringing an unrecognized religion into the city. Despite this law, prayer meetings persisted. The Jews created a place to steal away in secret prayer located more than a mile from the city's gate. Acts 16:13 informs us that this prayer meeting, located by the riverside, consisted of all women before Paul and his companions arrived.

Likewise our enslaved ancestors often had to gather in secret worship. In fact the Negro spiritual "Steal Away" was birthed through this practice. John Wesley Work in *Folk Song of the American Negro* recounts that on a certain plantation in the early 1800s, the slaves would cross the Red River to worship with the Indians. When forbidden to attend these services, the slaves decided to "steal away to Jesus," as one slave expressed it. On the day of the prayer service they would whisper the code "steal away to Jesus" in the fields throughout the day to signal that evening's meeting. And similar to the situation in Acts 16, assuredly the women were great in number at these clandestine meetings.

The sisters—often laden with yesterday's pain, today's burden, and tomorrow's gloom—had to steal away to Jesus for comfort and strength. And since they had stumbled so low in despair, the only place to fall was in the hopeful arms of Jesus. The women were often the ones who created a way to steal away. In Alex Haley's *Roots*, when Matilda, a God-fearing woman, discovered that prayer meetings were not held regularly, she "proposed that one be made a part of each Sunday afternoon." Matilda devised a way for her and the community to commune with God.

Is there a situation in your life that is obstructing your faith, thwarting your self-esteem, suppressing your hope, hindering your joy, or disallowing God's intended purposes for you? If so, you too must steal away to Jesus. When you lay your burdens before the Lord, it does not matter who says, "You can't." God will grant you renewed faith to continue, steadfast, in both your worship with and service for him.

(No prayer is written for this meditation. Take this time—wherever you are and in your own words—to steal away to Jesus. You can offer a prayer of praise, confession, thanksgiving, or supplication. Commune with the Lord according to your need.)

(KFW)

PRAYER CONCERN: First-time mothers

He maketh the barren women to keep house, and to be a joyful mother of children. Praise ye the Lord (Psalm 113:9, KJV).

PRAYER CONCERN: Single mothers

Be strong and courageous. Do not be terrified; do not be discouraged, for the Lord your God will be with you wherever you go (Josh. 1:9, NIV).

PRAYER CONCERN: Grandmothers

I have been reminded of your sincere faith, which first lived in your grandmother Lois and in your mother Eunice and, I am persuaded, now lives in you also (2 Tim. 1:5, NIV).

PRAYER CONCERN: Godmothers, foster mothers, and other guardians

Train up a child in the way he should go: and when he is old, he will not depart from it (Prov. 22:6, KJV).

PRAYER CONCERN: Bereaved mothers
My soul melts away for sorrow; strengthen me
according to your word (Psalm 119:28, NRSV).

PRAYER CONCERN: Mothers-in-law
[Treat] older women as mothers
(1 Tim. 5:-2a, NIV).

PRAYER CONCERN: Homeless mothers

May 7

The angel of God called to Hagar from heaven and said to her, "What is the matter, Hagar? Do not be afraid; God has heard the boy crying as he lies there. . . . I will make him into a great nation" (Gen. 21:17-18, NIV).

The quilt was a prayer of poor women. . . . They didn't have anything else to cover their children with.

— John Biggers

PRAYER CONCERN: Stepmothers

May 8

Then [Jesus] took a child and had him stand in front of them. He put his arms around him and said to them, "Whoever welcomes in my name one of these children, welcomes me; and whoever welcomes me, welcomes not only me but also the one who sent me" (Mark 9:36-37, TEV).

PRAYER CONCERN: Abused women

"For I know the plans I have for you," declares the Lord, "plans to prosper you and not to harm you, plans to give you hope and a future" (Jer. 29:11, NIV).

PRAYER CONCERN: Incarcerated mothers

"Come now, let us reason together," says the Lord. "Though your sins are like scarlet, they shall be as white as snow" (Isa. 1:18, NIV).

PRAYER CONCERN: Mothers with fulltime jobs

Fear thou not; for I am with thee: be not dismayed; for I am thy God: I will strengthen thee; yea, I will help thee; yea, I will uphold thee with the right hand of my righteousness (Isa. 41:10, KJV).

May 11

May 12

PRAYER CONCERN: Single Christian women who desire marriage

He who finds a wife finds a good thing, and obtains favor from the Lord (Prov. 18:22, NRSV).

May 13

PRAYER CONCERN: Women healing from a divorce

Jesus said, "I will not leave you comfortless: I will come to you" (John 14:18, KJV).

Indeed, because I first overheard my mother's praise and prayer in the rhythms of her song, and because I first overheard the praise and prayers of others like her, I was later able to hear the voice of God.

— Kenneth L. Waters Sr.

May 14

PRAYER CONCERN: Expectant mothers

Lo, children are an heritage of the Lord: and the fruit of the womb is his reward (Psalm 127:3, KJV).

PRAYER CONCERN: Codependent women

See to it that no one takes you captive through hollow and deceptive philosophy, which depends on human tradition and the basic principles of this world rather than on Christ (Col. 2:8, NIV).

PRAYER CONCERN: Women with low self-esteem

In all these things we are more than conquerors through [Christ] that loved us (Rom. 8:37, KJV).

PRAYER CONCERN: Women seeking employment

This is the assurance we have in approaching God: that if we ask anything according to his will, he hears us. And if we know that he hears us—whatever we ask—we know that we have what we asked of him (1 John 5:14-15, NIV).

PRAYER CONCERN: Resolution of mother-daughter conflicts

Get rid of all bitterness, rage and anger, brawling and slander, along with every form of malice. Be kind and compassionate to one another, forgiving each other, just as in Christ God forgave you (Eph. 4:31-32, NIV).

PRAYER CONCERN: Homemakers

She looketh well to the ways of her household,
and eateth not the bread of idleness
(Prov. 31:27, KJV).

PRAYER CONCERN: Women executives

I am the Lord your God, who teaches you
for your own good, who leads you in the way
you should go (Isa. 48:17*b*, NRSV).

May 21

PRAYER CONCERN: Widows

Religion that is pure and undefiled before God, the Father, is this: to care for orphans and widows in their distress, and to keep oneself unstained by the world (James 1:27, NRSV).

We must be persistent in prayer. We cannot afford the luxury of praying one time and then giving up. If an unrighteous judge will listen to and grant the request of a poor, defenseless widow [Luke 18:1-8], surely a just God will grant the requests of often unworthy but persistent children.

— Marjorie L. Kimbrough

May 22

PRAYER CONCERN: Women who feel abandoned

You shall no more be termed Forsaken, and your land shall no more be termed Desolate; but you shall be called My Delight Is in Her . . . for the Lord delights in you (Isa. 62:4, NRSV).

PRAYER CONCERN: Women who are financially compulsive

For the grace of God has appeared, bringing salvation to all, training us to renounce impiety and worldly passions, and in the present age to live lives that are self-controlled, upright, and godly (Titus 2:11, NRSV).

PRAYER CONCERN: Women reentering the work force

Jesus said, "The Helper, the Holy Spirit, whom the Father will send in my name, will teach you everything and make you remember all that I have told you" (John 14:26, TEV).

PRAYER CONCERN: Women in unhealthy relationships

Do not give what is holy to dogs—they will only turn and attack you. Do not throw your pearls in front of pigs—they will only trample them underfoot (Matt. 7:6, TEV).

PRAYER CONCERN: Women who abuse children

Wash away all my evil and make me clean from my sin! . . . I have sinned against you (Psalm 51:2, 4*a*, TEV).

PRAYER CONCERN: Women experiencing midlife crisis

The Lord said, "My grace is all you need; for my power is greatest when you are weak" (2 Cor. 12:9, TEV).

May
27

In my trials, Lord,
walk with me;
When my heart is
almost breaking,
Lord, I want Jesus
to walk with me.

—Negro Spiritual

PRAYER CONCERN: Emotionally stressed women

Find rest, O my soul, in God alone; my hope comes from him. He alone is my rock and my salvation; he is my fortress, I will not be shaken (Psalm 62:5-6, NIV).

May
28

PRAYER CONCERN: Godly womanhood

Favour is deceitful, and beauty is vain:
but a woman that feareth the Lord, she shall
be praised (Prov. 31:30, KJV).

PRAYER CONCERN: Women who live alone

The Lord will keep you from all harm—he will
watch over your life (Psalm 121:7, NIV).

PRAYER CONCERN: A woman who is an inspiration to you

She speaks with wisdom, and faithful instruction is on her tongue (Prov. 31:26, NIV).

A LITTLE TALK WITH JESUS

Chorus:
O a little talk with Jesus makes it right, all right,
Little talk with Jesus makes it right, all right,
Troubles of ev'ry kind, Thank God I'll always find
That a little talk with Jesus makes it right.

My brother, I remember when I was a sinner lost,
I cried, "Have mercy, Jesus," but still my soul
was tossed,
Till I heard King Jesus say, "Come here, I am
the way";
And a little talk with Jesus makes it right.

Sometimes the forked lightning and muttering
thunder, too,
Of trials and temptations make it hard for me
and you,
But Jesus is our friend, He'll keep us to the end;
And a little talk with Jesus makes it right.

My brother and my sister, you have trials here
like me,
When we are trying to serve the Lord, And win
the victory,
Old Satan fights us hard, Our journey to retard;
But a little talk with Jesus makes it right.

JUNE

PRAYERS
FOR
MEN

Discovering What Happens When Black Men Pray

Most Christian men pray like wimps and brag like warriors. The truth is that real spiritual warriors are men who pray.

— T. D. JAKES

ONE OF MY CHILDHOOD memories is seeing Black men pray at the Mount Zion Baptist Church in Akron, Ohio. After witnessing these men of prayer, I am convinced that something supernatural happens for the glory of God in the home, the church, and the community when Black men pray.

In the home Black men must pray to be effective as we take the leadership to meet the needs of the family. Our prayers must be fervent so that we may set the example for our children to see God at work. Taking the initiative to bring the family together for devotional time with God is paramount for Christian men. There is a spirit of love and cooperation when men pray in the home, and the unity of the family and marriage is strengthened. The homes of single men become Christ-centered too as they seek God's presence and purpose.

In the church as well, Christian men can bring a sense of empowerment to the congregation as we "have a little talk with Jesus." Men who are active in the prayer ministry, for example, can encourage other men to pray and not give up. Jesus taught in Luke 18:1 that "men ought to pray and not lose heart" (NKJV). T. D. Jakes is correct when he writes, "Real spiritual warriors are men who pray." I remember the prayers of my pastor, the Reverend I. T. Bradley. When he prayed, the congregation, especially the youth, felt empowered by God to stand. Rev. Bradley's prayers gave me and other youth courage to organize a protest march to secure jobs in a downtown department store. Rev. Bradley prayed with us and God opened the way for youth to be employed.

Something powerful also happens in the Black community when men pray. God gives these men stamina to take action and to transform their community. The Reverend Leon H. Sullivan, founder of Opportunities Industrialization Center, needed to begin a training program to prepare Black people for employment. Rev. Sullivan and his assistants not only needed teachers, they also needed knowledge regarding how to begin this training program. So he prayed. God answered his prayer through the words of Exodus 4:2: "What is that in thine hand?" (KJV). Rev. Sullivan and his close assistants began to use what they had in their hands—their own gifts and talents—and started a training program that produced results. They trained people for jobs that provided them a better future.

Christian brothers, we make a difference when we pray. We unify our homes, empower our churches, and transform our communities. Let us, then, become prayer warriors and make "a little talk with Jesus" a priority in our lives. And we will be amazed as we discover what happens!

PRAYER: Heavenly Father, help Christian Black brothers become praying men. Fill us with your spirit to pray and not lose heart. Make us effective for your glory not only in the home, church, and community, but wherever we are. This I pray, in the name of Jesus. Amen.
(LPT)

PRAYER CONCERN: To be godly men

But you, man of God . . . pursue righteousness, godliness, faith, love, endurance, and gentleness. Fight the good fight of the faith (1 Tim. 6:11-12*a*, NIV).

PRAYER CONCERN: To be godly fathers

Hear, my children, the instruction of a father, and give attention to know understanding (Prov. 4:1, NKJV).

PRAYER CONCERN: For grandfathers, godfathers, and guardians

Children's children are the crown of old men, and the glory of children is their father (Prov. 17:6, NKJV).

June

3

PRAYER CONCERN: To lead the family in daily devotions

I have chosen [Abraham], that he may charge his children and his household after him to keep the way of the Lord by doing righteousness and justice (Gen. 18:19*a*, NRSV).

June

4

**PRAYER CONCERN: To find joy
in work well done**

A man can do nothing better than to eat and
drink and find satisfaction in his work
(Eccles. 2:24, NIV).

**PRAYER CONCERN: For men to bond
and be supportive**

Iron sharpeneth iron; so a man sharpeneth the
countenance of his friend (Prov. 27:17, KJV).

PRAYER CONCERN: For healing of unresolved emotional issues

Behold, I will bring it health and healing; I will heal them and reveal to them the abundance of peace and truth (Jer. 33:6, NKJV).

June
7

Prayer puts beauty on our faces because it puts serenity and peace in our lives.

— Gardner C. Taylor

PRAYER CONCERN: For bereaved fathers

Be merciful to me, O Lord, for I am in distress; my eyes grow weak with sorrow, and my soul and my body with grief (Psalm 31:9, NIV).

June
8

June 9

PRAYER CONCERN: For men who are incarcerated

I needed clothes and you clothed me, I was sick and you looked after me, I was in prison and you came to visit me (Matt. 25:36, NIV).

June 10

PRAYER CONCERN: For loyalty in marriage

Nevertheless let each one of you in particular so love his wife even as himself, and let the wife see that she respects her husband (Eph. 5:33 NKJV).

PRAYER CONCERN: For opportunities to advance in the workplace

June
11

David said, "So be strong, show yourself a man, and observe what the Lord your God requires: Walk in his ways, and keep his decrees and commands, his laws and requirements, . . . so that you may prosper in all you do and wherever you go" (1 Kings 2:2*b*-3, NIV).

PRAYER CONCERN: Healing for men who have divorced

June
12

Then they cried out to the Lord in their trouble, and He saved them out of their distresses (Psalm 107:19, NKJV).

June

13

PRAYER CONCERN: For men who are changing careers

Whatsoever thy hand findeth to do, do it with thy might (Eccles. 9:10, KJV).

Have you prayed about that decision? Have you asked God to show you what He wants you to do? He promised that He would. Sometimes we don't know God's will simply because we have not taken time to ask Him.

— Crawford W. Loritts

June

14

PRAYER CONCERN: For men seeking direction

Your ears shall hear a word behind you, saying, "This is the way, walk in it," whenever you turn to the right hand or whenever you turn to the left (Isa. 30:21, NKJV).

**PRAYER CONCERN: For men whose
wives have died**

Blessed are they that mourn: for they shall
be comforted (Matt. 5:4, KJV).

**PRAYER CONCERN: For men who
have been sexually abused**

Have mercy upon me, O Lord; for I am weak:
O Lord, heal me; for my bones are vexed
(Psalm 6:2, KJV).

June 17

PRAYER CONCERN: For men seeking employment

Ask and it will be given to you; seek and you will find; knock and the door will be opened to you (Matt. 7:7, NIV).

June 18

PRAYER CONCERN: To overcome failure

It is the Lord who goes before you. He will be with you; he will not fail you or forsake you. Do not fear or be dismayed (Deut. 31:8, NRSV).

PRAYER CONCERN: For fathers who have forsaken their parental responsibilities

For I acknowledge my transgressions: and my sin is ever before me (Psalm 51:3, KJV).

June
19

PRAYER CONCERN: For men who need help handling finances

Wealth hastily gotten will dwindle, but those who gather little by little will increase it (Prov. 13:11, NRSV).

June
20

**June
21**

**PRAYER CONCERN: For spirit-filled leadership
in the men's ministry**

Therefore, friends, select from among yourselves
seven men of good standing, full of the Spirit
and of wisdom, whom we may appoint to
this task (Acts 6:3, NRSV).

*The praisers of men
are not excited about
prayer warriors. They
love great preachers,
but they don't
acknowledge great
men of prayer.*

— T. D. Jakes

**June
22**

PRAYER CONCERN: For men who are indecisive

When he asks, he must believe and not doubt,
because he who doubts is like a wave of the sea,
blown and tossed by the wind (James 1:6, NIV).

PRAYER CONCERN: For home ownership

Unless the Lord builds the house, those who build it labor in vain (Psalm 127:1, NRSV).

PRAYER CONCERN: Morning prayer for men

And in [Daniel's] upper room, with his windows open toward Jerusalem, he knelt down on his knees three times that day, and prayed and gave thanks before his God, as was his custom since early days (Dan. 6:10*b-c*, NKJV).

June 25

PRAYER CONCERN: Noon prayer for men

About noon the following day as they were approaching the city, Peter went up on the roof to pray (Acts 10:9, NIV).

June 26

PRAYER CONCERN: Evening prayer for men

One of those days Jesus went out into the hills to pray, and spent the night praying to God (Luke 6:12, NIV).

PRAYER CONCERN: For more Christian Black men to be active in the church

Serve the Lord with gladness (Psalm 100:2, KJV).

To pastors and fellow believers, my prayer is that you will search within your souls and design churches and develop ministries that will be influential in bringing African American males to Christ.

— Jawanza Kunjufu

PRAYER CONCERN: For husbands to love their wives

Husbands, love your wives and do not be bitter toward them (Col. 3:19, NKJV).

June

29

**PRAYER CONCERN: For men who desire
to become entrepreneurs**

And the Lord answered me, and said, Write
the vision, and make it plain upon tables, that
he may run that readeth it (Hab. 2:2, KJV).

June

30

**PRAYER CONCERN: For men who fear
the unknown**

I sought the Lord, and he answered me;
he delivered me from all my fears
(Psalm 34:4, NIV).

© Jean-Claude Lejeune

KUM BA YAH, MY LORD

Kum ba yah, my Lord, Kum ba yah.
Kum ba yah, my Lord, Kum ba yah.
Kum ba yah, my Lord, Kum ba yah.
Oh, Lord,_ Kum ba yah.

Someone's cryin', Lord, Kum ba yah.
Someone's cryin', Lord, Kum ba yah.
Someone's cryin', Lord, Kum ba yah.
Oh, Lord,_ Kum ba yah.

Someone's singin', Lord, Kum ba yah.
Someone's singin', Lord, Kum ba yah.
Someone's singin', Lord, Kum ba yah.
Oh, Lord,_ Kum ba yah.

Someone's prayin', Lord, Kum ba yah.
Someone's prayin', Lord, Kum ba yah.
Someone's prayin', Lord, Kum ba yah.
Oh, Lord,_ Kum ba yah.

Someone needs you, Lord, Kum ba yah.
Someone needs you, Lord, Kum ba yah.
Someone needs you, Lord, Kum ba yah.
Oh, Lord,_ Kum ba yah.

JULY

PRAYERS
FOR
CHILDREN
AND
YOUTH

Setting Our Children Free

Through the power of the Spirit,
let's empower each other
to go out with power
to set all the children free.
— JAMES FORBES, JR.

MY SUNDAY SCHOOL students and I were discussing expectations one Sunday morning. "What should be our class rules?" I asked the group, who ranged in age from seven to twelve. "What should I expect from you?" The students made a list of well-honored rules, which included respecting one another, coming to class on time, and not using profanity. I also added my rules. Then I reversed the question and asked, "What are your expectations of me as your teacher?" Ten-year-old Kim challenged: "We expect you to tell us the truth." Kim's words made a profound impression on me.

As I taught my class for the next two and a half years, I often thought about Kim and during my lesson preparations I would ask, "Lord, am I teaching truth here?"

Our children and youth need people who will tell them the truth. More than twenty years ago John M. Drescher wrote *Seven Things Children Need*. These basic needs included God, discipline, love, praise, acceptance, security, and significance. Drescher's book, though dated, is quite applicable for today.

Just think about what happens to our youth when godly truth is absent. When we do not discipline a child in truth, for example, we fluctuate between being abusive and being too permissive. And Drescher states that over-permissiveness produces insecurity in the child. Or if we are always telling a child, "You are stupid and worthless," then that child develops low self-esteem, and this untruth hinders the child from living out his or her full potential. So the absence of truth erodes children's mental, emotional, and physical health, forcing them to carry emotional baggage that engenders bondage, not freedom.

In John 8:32, Jesus offers freedom by way of truth: "You shall know the truth, and the truth shall make you free" (NKJV). We are able to obtain this freedom by having a relationship with Jesus—the one who is the way and the truth. As we are empowered and liberated through truths of the gospel, we can thus empower our children in our homes and communities.

Let us cultivate our devotional life and allow God to nurture truth within us. This truth, as the Gospel of John promises, will produce the bountiful harvest of freedom— freedom for us, our children, and their descendants.

PRAYER: Dear Lord, remove falsehood and deception from us, and create in us a desire to be truthful and sincere. Help us use your word to live these truths and to deposit them into the lives of young people everywhere. Amen.

(KFW)

PRAYER CONCERN: Teenage parents

Unto thee, O Lord, do I lift up my soul. O my God, I trust in thee: let me not be ashamed (Psalm 25:1-2, KJV).

PRAYER CONCERN: Christian teens

May our Lord Jesus Christ himself and God our Father, who loved us and in his grace gave us unfailing courage and firm hope, encourage you and strengthen you to always do and say what is good (2 Thess. 2:16-17, TEV).

PRAYER CONCERN: Those in gangs

Evil men understand not judgment: but they
that seek the Lord understand all things
(Prov. 28:5, KJV).

PRAYER CONCERN: High-school dropouts

Do not forsake wisdom, and she will protect you;
love her, and she will watch over you
(Prov. 4:6, NIV).

PRAYER CONCERN: Rebellious children and youth

Children, obey your parents in everything, for this is your acceptable duty in the Lord (Col. 3:20, NRSV).

PRAYER CONCERN: Teenagers with low self-esteem

Are not two sparrows sold for a penny? Yet not one of them will fall to the ground apart from your Father. And even the hairs of your head are all counted. So do not be afraid; you are of more value than many sparrows (Matt. 10:29-31, NRSV).

PRAYER CONCERN: Undisciplined children

Do not withhold discipline from a child; if you punish him with the rod, he will not die (Prov. 23:13, NIV).

I don't view it [advocating for children] as a job. I view it as a mission. . . . Without faith, without prayer, I certainly couldn't continue the struggle day after day and year after year.

— Marian Wright Edelman

PRAYER CONCERN: Christian role models for children and youth

Paul said, "Brothers and sisters, join in imitating me, and observe those who live according to the example you have in us" (Phil. 3:17, NRSV).

PRAYER CONCERN: Teens on drugs

Be very careful, then, how you live—not as unwise but as wise, making the most of every opportunity, because the days are evil. Therefore do not be foolish, but understand what the Lord's will is (Eph. 5:15-17, NIV).

PRAYER CONCERN: Children awaiting adoption

Seek justice, rescue the oppressed, defend the orphan, plead for the widow (Isa. 1:17*b-c*, NRSV).

PRAYER CONCERN: Latchkey children

For he shall give his angels charge over thee, to keep thee in all thy ways (Psalm 91:11, KJV).

PRAYER CONCERN: Sexually abused children

Rise up, O Lord; O God, lift up your hand; do not forget the oppressed (Psalm 10:12, NRSV).

July 13

PRAYER CONCERN: Incarcerated youth

God has shown us how much he loves us—
it was while we were still sinners that Christ
died for us! (Rom. 5:8, TEV)

*Whenever we talk
about being advocates
for children, we must
begin with prayer.*
— Holding Children
in Prayer

July 14

PRAYER CONCERN: Neglected children

Speak up for those who cannot speak for
themselves (Prov. 31:8, NIV).

PRAYER CONCERN: Children in custody battles

For in the day of trouble [God] will keep me safe in his dwelling; he will hide me in the shelter of his tabernacle and set me high upon a rock (Psalm 27:5, NIV).

PRAYER CONCERN: Children and youth with disabilities

I myself will be the shepherd of my sheep. . . . I will bind up the injured, and I will strengthen the weak (Ezek. 34:15a,16b, NRSV).

PRAYER CONCERN: Juvenile delinquents
The way of a fool seems right to him, but
a wise man listens to advice (Prov. 12:15, NIV).

PRAYER CONCERN: Teens and peer pressure
Do not be fooled. "Bad companions ruin
good character" (1 Cor. 15:33, TEV).

PRAYER CONCERN: Children adjusting to stepfamilies

As a mother comforts her child, so will [the Lord] comfort you (Isa. 66:13, NIV).

July
19

PRAYER CONCERN: Children grieving the death of a parent

For the Lord comforts his people and will have compassion on his afflicted ones (Isa. 49:13*b*, NIV).

July
20

July 21

PRAYER CONCERN: Children and youth seeking God

Jesus said, "Let the little children come to me, and do not hinder them, for the kingdom of heaven belongs to such as these" (Matt. 19:14, NIV).

I remembered the impressions that had been made upon me, when a child, at the prayer meetings that had been held in the house of my parents. Those religious impressions . . . were like grain that is sown, and continues to grow until it has arrived at full perfection.

— Daniel H. Peterson

July 22

PRAYER CONCERN: Refugee children in various countries

[The Lord,] who executes justice for the oppressed; who gives food to the hungry (Psalm 146:7*b*, NRSV).

PRAYER CONCERN: Children grieving the death of a sibling

Relieve the troubles of my heart, and bring me out of my distress (Psalm 25:17, NRSV).

July 23

PRAYER CONCERN: Teens who have run away from home

Search me, O God, and know my heart; test me and know my thoughts. See if there is any wicked way in me, and lead me in the way everlasting (Psalm 139:23-24, NRSV).

July 24

PRAYER CONCERN: Persons who work with the Big Brothers/Big Sisters organizations

Pray to the owner of the harvest that he will send out workers to gather in his harvest (Matt. 9:38, TEV).

PRAYER CONCERN: Teens who have recently received a driver's license

The Lord bless you and keep you (Num. 6:24, NIV).

**PRAYER CONCERN: Children and youth
in support groups**

When I thought, "My foot is slipping," your steadfast love, O Lord, held me up. When the cares of my heart are many, your consolations cheer my soul (Psalm 94:18-19, NRSV).

July
27

Mom says, "Good night." She turns off the light. My room is dark. Is there something under the bed? Or somebody in the closet? Help! I'm scared! That's when I talk to God.

— Patricia and
Fredrick McKissack

**PRAYER CONCERN: Young persons seeking
direction regarding college**

I will instruct thee and teach thee in the way which thou shalt go: I will guide thee with mine eye (Psalm 32:8, KJV).

July
28

PRAYER CONCERN: Children whose parents have joint custody

You, O Lord, will protect us
(Psalm 12:7a, NRSV).

PRAYER CONCERN: A young person who feels hopeless

Why are you downcast, O my soul? Why so disturbed within me? Put your hope in God, for I will yet praise him, my Savior and my God (Psalm 42:5, NIV).

PRAYER CONCERN: A specific way to reach out to children in your community

So Jesus called a child to come and stand in front of them, and said, "I assure you that unless you change and become like children, you will never enter the Kingdom of heaven" (Matt. 18:2-3, TEV).

KING JESUS IS A-LISTENIN'

Chorus:
King Jesus is a-listenin' all day long,
King Jesus is a-listenin' all day long,
King Jesus is a-listenin' all day long,
To hear some sinner pray.

Some say that John the Baptist
Was nothin' but a Jew,
But the Holy Bible tells us
That John was a preacher too.

That Gospel train is comin',
A-rum-blin through the lan',
But I hear them wheels a hum-min',
Get ready to board that train!

I know I been converted,
I ain't gon' make no alarm,
For my soul is bound for Glory,
And the devil can't do me no harm.

AUGUST

PRAYERS
FOR THE
FAMILY

Hearing a Word from the Lord

Don't you do it, honey; wait, . . . let me take
one of de Lord's scrolls an' read it to you.
— AN ELDER SLAVE WOMAN

A MOTHER IN TENNESSEE, sold to a slave owner in Mississippi, would soon have to face the torture of parting with her baby girl. Though the pain of separation was unbearable enough, conditions for slaves in Mississippi were worse. Between her living conditions and the prospect of separation from her child, the mother's anguish was so intolerable that she decided to drown both herself and her child in the Cumberland River.

The mother placed the child on her breast and headed to the river. At about the same time an older slave woman saw the mother, rushed toward her, placed her hand on the mother's shoulder, and said: "Don't you do it, honey; wait, . . . let me take one of de Lord's scrolls an' read it to you." The older woman then pretended to unroll a scroll and said, "God's got a great work for dis baby to do; she's gon' to stand befo' kings and queens. Don't you do it, honey." These words so stirred the heart of the mother that she abandoned her suicidal mission. Because that mother, known as Sarah Hannah Sheppard, hearkened to her elder's prophetic words, years later her daughter, Ella, enrolled at Fisk University and became one of the original Jubilee Singers. Ella Sheppard Moore indeed sang before royalty as the group toured Europe.

In the midst of distress Sister Sheppard heard a word from the Lord for her family that altered her destiny and produced the blessings of life instead of the afflictions of a premature death.

160

Families today also suffer from the woes of fragmentation and societal ills—spousal abuse, drug addiction, negligent and abusive parents, racial discrimination—the record of adversities goes on. Families need a word from the Lord. We can offer this word by saturating our homes with prayer—praying for and with our families—and by using the Bible as our guideline for living.

We learn from the slave mother that we do not only need to hear a word, but in order to be effective we must also heed the word. By adhering to biblical principles we receive God's blessings. Deuteronomy 28:2-3 states, "All these blessings will come upon you and accompany you if you obey the Lord your God: You will be blessed in the city and blessed in the country" (NIV). Mother Sheppard surely reaped a blessing. She was reunited with Ella years later and lived in her daughter's beautiful home.

Even hearing and heeding are not the conclusion of the matter. We must also speak a word to our children, spouses, sisters, brothers, mothers, fathers, and our host of relatives to bring healing and wholeness. One day the word might be: "Press on daughter; with the Lord's help, you'll make it" (after Romans 15:13). Another hour we may say, "Son, God has given you the ability, now go boldly" (after Philippians 4:13). During one moment we may utter, "Mother, our God will provide" (after Genesis 22:8). And on numerous occasions we may lovingly voice, "Don't you do it, honey; wait."

PRAYER: My God, help me to hear a word from one of your servants, to heed to godly counsel, and to speak words of wisdom to a soul in distress.

(KFW)

August 1

PRAYER CONCERN: Newlyweds

For this reason a man will leave his father and mother and be united to his wife, and they will become one flesh (Gen. 2:24, NIV).

August 2

PRAYER CONCERN: Interracial marriages

Let love and faithfulness never leave you . . . write them on the tablet of your heart (Prov. 3:3*a,c*, NIV).

PRAYER CONCERN: Military families

Preserve me, O God: for in thee do I put
my trust (Psalm 16:1 KJV).

**PRAYER CONCERN: Persons attending
family reunions**

How very good and pleasant it is when kindred
live together in unity! (Psalm 133:1, NRSV)

August 5

PRAYER CONCERN: Dissension among family members

Bear with one another and, if anyone has a complaint against another, forgive each other; just as the Lord has forgiven you, so you also must forgive. Above all clothe yourselves with love, which binds everything together in perfect harmony (Col. 3:13-14, NRSV).

August 6

PRAYER CONCERN: Safety for families on vacation

Blessed shall you be when you come in, and blessed shall you be when you go out (Deut. 28:6, NRSV).

PRAYER CONCERN: Families seeking home ownership

August
7

The Lord will send a blessing on your barns and on everything you put your hand to. The Lord your God will bless you in the land he is giving you (Deut. 28:8, NIV).

Heavenly Father, help me to make my home as special and sacred as heaven. Let it be built by wisdom, knowledge, and pleasant riches. Establish my home with reverence and obedience to you, God. . . . This I pray. Amen.

— Lloyd Preston
Terrell

PRAYER CONCERN: Senior citizens who have been crime victims

August
8

I will exult and rejoice in your steadfast love, because you have seen my affliction; you have taken heed of my adversities (Psalm 31:7, NRSV).

PRAYER CONCERN: Couples who argue constantly

Finally, all of you, live in harmony with one another; be sympathetic . . . be compassionate and humble. Do not repay evil with evil or insult with insult, but with blessing, because to this you were called so that you might inherit a blessing (1 Peter 3:8-9, NIV).

PRAYER CONCERN: Blended families

Happy is everyone who fears the Lord. . . . Your wife will be like a fruitful vine within your house; your children will be like olive shoots around your table. Thus shall the man be blessed who fears the Lord (Psalm 128:1, 3-4, NRSV).

PRAYER CONCERN: Healing of broken relationships among family members

You must see that justice is done, and must show kindness and mercy to one another (Zech. 7:9*b*, TEV).

PRAYER CONCERN: Married couples who desire to have a child

Because Rebecca had no children, Isaac prayed to the Lord for her. The Lord answered his prayer, and Rebecca became pregnant (Gen. 25:21, TEV).

August

13

PRAYER CONCERN: Spouses with jobs that require frequent travel

God knows that I always remember you every time I pray (Rom. 1:9*b*, TEV).

Every day before supper, and before we went to services on Sundays, my grandmother would read the Bible to me, and my grandfather would pray. . . . Prayer and the Bible became a part of my everyday thoughts and beliefs.

— Rosa Parks

August

14

PRAYER CONCERN: A godly family heritage

Posterity will serve him; future generations will be told about the Lord. They will proclaim his righteousness to a people yet unborn—for he has done it (Psalm 22:30-31, NIV).

PRAYER CONCERN: Persons caring for an elderly parent

The Lord will give strength unto his people; the Lord will bless his people with peace (Psalm 29:11, KJV).

PRAYER CONCERN: Parents who lack parenting skills

But if any of you lacks wisdom, you should pray to God, who will give it to you; because God gives generously and graciously to all (James 1:5, TEV).

August 17

PRAYER CONCERN: **Nursing-home patients**

Truly the eye of the Lord is on those who fear him, on those who hope in his steadfast love (Psalm 33:18, NRSV).

August 18

PRAYER CONCERN: **Elderly persons who live alone**

Peace I leave with you, my peace I give unto you: not as the world giveth, give I unto you. Let not your heart be troubled, neither let it be afraid (John 14:27, KJV).

PRAYER CONCERN: Elderly persons experiencing financial struggles

Even to your old age and gray hairs I am [the Lord], I am he who will sustain you. I have made you and I will carry you; I will sustain you and I will rescue you (Isa. 46:4, NIV).

August **19**

PRAYER CONCERN: Senior citizens who are rearing young children

She stretcheth out her hand to the poor; yea, she reacheth forth her hands to the needy (Prov. 31:20, KJV).

August **20**

PRAYER CONCERN: Families suffering financial difficulty

But my God shall supply all your need according to his riches in glory by Christ Jesus (Phil. 4:19, KJV).

Prayer is a real eye-opener because it opens our eyes to the reality of God's presence in all of life's circumstances.

— Kevin W. Cosby

PRAYER CONCERN: Your family's needs

If ye abide in me, and my words abide in you, ye shall ask what ye will, and it shall be done unto you (John 15:7, KJV).

PRAYER CONCERN: Parents who have special-needs children

"The Lord is my portion," says my soul, "therefore I will hope in him" (Lam. 3:24, NRSV).

August 23

PRAYER CONCERN: Marriages that need revitalizing

Now to him who by the power at work within us is able to accomplish abundantly far more than we can ask or imagine, to him be glory in the church and in Christ Jesus to all generations, forever and ever. Amen (Eph. 3:20-21, NRSV).

August 24

PRAYER CONCERN: Families with missing children

When anxiety was great within me, your consolation brought joy to my soul. . . . But the Lord has become my fortress, and my God the rock in whom I take refuge (Psalm 94:19, 22, NIV).

PRAYER CONCERN: Parents with critically ill children

The steadfast love of the Lord never ceases, his mercies never come to an end; they are new every morning; great is your faithfulness (Lam. 3:22-23, NRSV).

**PRAYER CONCERN: Persons caring
for a critically ill spouse**

Blessed be God, which hath not turned away
my prayer, nor his mercy from me
(Psalm 66:20, KJV).

August
27

*I'm always amazed at
the power of prayer.*
— Bessie Delany

**PRAYER CONCERN: Parents who spend
too little time with their children**

Parents, do not treat your children in such a
way as to make them angry. Instead, raise
them with Christian discipline and instruction
(Eph. 6:4, TEV).

August
28

August 29

PRAYER CONCERN: Guidance for persons preparing living wills

Walk about Zion . . . that you may tell the next generation that this is God, our God forever and ever. He will be our guide forever (Psalm 48:12*a*, 13*b*-14, NRSV).

August 30

PRAYER CONCERN: Families who have recently moved to a new city

But the Lord is faithful, who shall stablish you, and keep you from evil (2 Thess. 3:3, KJV).

PRAYER CONCERN: Offer thanks to God for your family

May my prayer be set before you like incense; may the lifting up of my hands be like the evening sacrifice (Psalm 141:2, NIV).

LORD, I WANT TO BE A CHRISTIAN

Lord, I want to be a Christian in my heart,
in my heart,
Lord, I want to be a Christian in my heart—
In my heart, in my heart,
Lord, I want to be a Christian in my heart.

Lord, I want to be more loving in my heart,
in my heart,
Lord, I want to be more loving in my heart—
In my heart, in my heart,
Lord, I want to be more loving in my heart.

Lord, I want to be more holy in my heart,
in my heart,
Lord, I want to be more holy in my heart—
In my heart, in my heart,
Lord, I want to be more holy in my heart.

Lord, I want to be like Jesus in my heart,
in my heart,
Lord, I want to be like Jesus in my heart—
In my heart, in my heart,
Lord, I want to be like Jesus in my heart.

SEPTEMBER

PRAYERS
FOR THE
EDUCATIONAL
SYSTEM

Mixing Prayers with Your Labors

*I am God's servant. . . . I am just the instrument
through which He speaks, and I would be able to do
more if I were to stay in close touch with Him. With
my prayers, I mix my labors, and sometimes God is
pleased to bless the results.*

— GEORGE WASHINGTON CARVER

GEORGE WASHINGTON CARVER was a devout Christian
and a brilliant educator. In the classroom and other public forums he often accredited his knowledge to divine
inspiration and guidance. He referred to his laboratory
as God's Little Workshop, and he considered himself an
instrument for God's use. In his day, newspaper articles
carried headlines that read "Chemist Attributes Success
to Divinity," "Negro Professor Aided by Heaven," "Gives
Credit to God," and "Colored Savant Credits Heaven."
Some were written to criticize the professor's faith. In one
article the writer stated, "Real chemists . . . do not ascribe
their successes, when they have any, to 'inspiration.' Talk
of that sort will simply bring ridicule."

Though criticisms of Professor Carver's mixing faith
and academics continued, he remained unmoved in his
beliefs. Through his actions, Carver maintained, as Jesus
stated, "I do nothing on my own but speak just what the
Father has taught me" (John 8:28*b*, NIV). And by hearing
God's voice Carver developed more than three hundred
products from the peanut, 118 products from the sweet
potato, and seventy-five products from the pecan.

We must encourage students and educators to be attentive to the voice of God. Teaching, dealing with racist teachers, coping with learning disabilities, counseling students, and confronting school violence can be challenging, laborious, and frightening. Offering our prayers to God will strengthen us, and at the same time bless our endeavors.

PRAYER: Lord, help our teachers, students, school administrators, and all persons in the educational system. Direct them to offer their educational goals and labors to you and become persons of prayer—instruments through which you speak. Grant them, O God, your anointing, direction, and strength to fulfill your will. Amen.

(KFW)

September 1

PRAYER CONCERN: **Principals**

Teach me good judgment and knowledge,
for I believe in your commandments
(Psalm 119:66, NRSV).

September 2

PRAYER CONCERN: **School secretaries**

But continue to grow in the grace and
knowledge of our Lord and Savior Jesus Christ
(2 Peter 3:18a, TEV).

PRAYER CONCERN: Parent-teacher organizations

That is why we always pray for you. We ask our God to make you worthy of the life he has called you to live. May he fulfill by his power all your desire for goodness and complete your work of faith (2 Thess. 1:11, TEV).

September 3

PRAYER CONCERN: School counselors

The wise in heart are called discerning, and pleasant words promote instruction. (Prov. 16:21, NIV).

September 4

September 5

PRAYER CONCERN: School psychologists
The Sovereign Lord has taught me what to say, so that I can strengthen the weary. Every morning he makes me eager to hear what he is going to teach me (Isa. 50:4-5, TEV).

September 6

PRAYER CONCERN: Safety for school-bus drivers
[The Lord] guards them all the day long, and he dwells in their midst (Deut. 33:12b, TEV).

PRAYER CONCERN: School superintendents

Wisdom is the principal thing; therefore get wisdom: and with all thy getting get understanding (Prov. 4:7, KJV).

September
7

Too often, we put faith at one end of the spectrum and wisdom at the other. But faithful folk ask for wisdom, and they do get it.

— Ella Pearson Mitchell

PRAYER CONCERN: School coaches

Keep yourself in training for a godly life. Physical exercise has some value, but spiritual exercise is valuable in every way, because it promises life both for the present and for the future (1 Tim. 4:7*b*-8, TEV).

September
8

September 9

PRAYER CONCERN: **Employees of before- and after-school programs**

Commit to the Lord whatever you do, and your plans will succeed (Prov. 16:3, NIV).

September 10

PRAYER CONCERN: **Elementary- and middle-school children**

My child, do not let these escape from your sight: keep sound wisdom and prudence, and they will be life for your soul (Prov. 3:21-22, NRSV).

PRAYER CONCERN: High-school students
Remember your creator in the days of your
youth (Eccles. 12:1, NRSV).

**PRAYER CONCERN: Funds for historically
Black colleges**
We will tell the next generation the praiseworthy
deeds of the Lord, his power and the wonders
he has done (Psalm 78:4*b-d*, NIV).

September
12

September

13

PRAYER CONCERN: College professors
In your teaching show integrity, seriousness and
soundness of speech that cannot be condemned
(Titus 2:7*b*, NIV).

Gracious God. . . .
Encourage each
teacher to look to you
for power to reach the
minds and hearts of
students. Let each day
in the classroom be
a blessed experience
which will produce a
great change in all of
our lives. This we pray
in your son Jesus'
name. Amen.

— Lloyd Preston
Terrell

September

14

**PRAYER CONCERN: Teachers and
teachers' assistants**
Trust in the Lord with all thine heart; and
lean not unto thine own understanding. In
all thy ways acknowledge him, and he shall
direct thy paths (Prov. 3:5-6, KJV).

PRAYER CONCERN: College students

Listen to what is wise and try to understand it. Yes, beg for knowledge; plead for insight. Look for it as hard as you would for silver or some hidden treasure. If you do, you will know what it means to fear the Lord and you will succeed in learning about God (Prov. 2:2-5, TEV).

September
15

PRAYER CONCERN: Day-care workers

Jesus said, "See that you do not look down on one of these little ones. For I tell you that their angels in heaven always see the face of my Father in heaven" (Matt. 18:10-11, NIV).

September
16

September 17

PRAYER CONCERN: Student athletes

Finally, be strong in the Lord and in the strength of his power (Eph. 6:10, NRSV).

September 18

PRAYER CONCERN: Home-schooled children and their parents

These commandments that I give you today are to be upon your hearts. Impress them on your children. Talk about them when you sit at home and when you walk along the road, when you lie down and when you get up (Deut. 6:6-7, NIV).

PRAYER CONCERN: Seminary students

Study to show thyself approved unto God, a workman that needeth not to be ashamed, rightly dividing the word of truth (2 Tim. 2:15, KJV).

September 19

PRAYER CONCERN: School violence

Have nothing to do with the fruitless deeds of darkness, but rather expose them (Eph. 5:11, NIV).

September 20

September 21

PRAYER CONCERN: Private Christian schools

Jesus said, "I am the light of the world. Whoever follows me will never walk in darkness, but will have the light of life" (John 8:12*b-c*, NIV).

Let others say what they will of the efficacy of prayer, I believe in it, and I shall pray. Thank God! Yes, I shall always pray.

— Sojourner Truth

September 22

PRAYER CONCERN: Students who need financial assistance

I was young and now I am old, yet I have never seen the righteous forsaken or their children begging bread (Psalm 37:25, NIV).

**PRAYER CONCERN: Direction for
high-school seniors**

[O Lord,] you hold me by my right hand.
You guide me with your counsel
(Psalm 73:23*b*-24, NIV).

September
23

**PRAYER CONCERN: School nurses and
social workers**

I am confident of this, that the one who began a
good work among you will bring it to completion
by the day of Jesus Christ (Phil. 1:6, NRSV).

September
24

September 25

PRAYER CONCERN: **Kindergartners**

He will cover you with his pinions, and under his wings you will find refuge (Psalm 91:4, NRSV).

September 26

PRAYER CONCERN: **Safety for children who walk to and from school**

Everyone knows how good you are, how securely you protect those who trust you. You hide them in the safety of your presence from the plots of others; in a safe shelter you hide them from the insults of their enemies (Psalm 31:19*b*-20, TEV).

PRAYER CONCERN: Persons enrolled in a literacy program

I can do all things through Christ which strengtheneth me (Phil. 4:13, KJV).

Prayer is much more than the words that we utter: Prayer is an attitude of openness to God. It is centering in, becoming present to God. It is being prepared for intimate conversation with the Creator.

— Robert E. Dungy

PRAYER CONCERN: Foreign students adjusting to American and Canadian schools

[The Lord] loves the foreigners who live with our people, and gives them food and clothes. So then, show love . . . because you were once foreigners in Egypt (Deut. 10:18*b*-19, TEV).

September 29

PRAYER CONCERN: **Safety for students studying abroad**

I will both lie down and sleep in peace; for you alone, O Lord, make me lie down in safety (Psalm 4:8, NRSV).

September 30

PRAYER CONCERN: **School volunteers, tutors**

In the same way, let your light shine before others, so that they may see your good works and give glory to your Father in heaven (Matt. 5:16, NRSV).

Richard Lord/© General Board of Global Ministries, The United Methodist Church

HE'S GOT THE WHOLE WORLD IN HIS HANDS

He's got the whole world in His hands,
He's got the big, round world in His hands,
He's got the whole world in His hands,
He's got the whole world in His hands,

He's got the wind and the rain in His hands,
He's got the wind and the rain in His hands,
He's got the wind and the rain in His hands,
He's got the whole world in His hands,

He's got the little bitty baby in His hands,
He's got the little bitty baby in His hands,
He's got the little bitty baby in His hands,
He's got the whole world in His hands,

He's got you and me, sister, in His hands,
He's got you and me, sister, in His hands,
He's got you and me, sister, in His hands,
He's got the whole world in His hands,

He's got you and me, brother, in His hands,
He's got you and me, brother, in His hands,
He's got you and me, brother, in His hands,
He's got the whole world in His hands,

OCTOBER

PRAYERS
FOR
INTERNATIONAL CONCERNS

Restoring World Order

God is calling nations of people, not races,
to repentance.
— BERNICE A. KING

THE WORLD IS NOT a hopeless place. It is our parish. Restoring the world to God's original intent is the ministry of every Christian. The world is depending on the prayers of the righteous for renewal and hope. Prayer is the wheel that turns our eyes, ears, and hearts toward God to listen for divine ways to bring a lost world back to God. Prayer keeps us seeing the best in humankind.

Genesis 1:31 says, "Then God saw everything that he had made, and indeed it was very good" (NIV). This scripture gives praying people a glimpse of God's holy will for the world. Everything that God created in the world was good! God created the world to be a beautiful and peaceful place. God created the world to be without war, hunger, racism, sexism, and classism. Our God created a world of divine order. Through prayer, Christians have the opportunity to call the world into repentance for the disorder that exists.

Sin is the root cause of the world's crumbling order. Restoring world order is a spiritual matter. Why have governments and world powers failed? Governments collapse solely from human frailty and the quest for power. Isaiah 9:6-7 tells us that God's plan for restoring world order comes through Jesus Christ. Jesus is the world's answer to arrogance, greed, and pride.

Black Christians must continue to pray for the world. We too are called by God to have a global perspective on prayer. God's global concern for the world transcends all barriers of color, sex, age, or economic status. God has the entire world in his hands. When we pray for restoring world order, we too are confessing God's power to change people who hate, people who oppress others, and people who do not share their wealth with the poor.

Since world evil is evident and systemic, prayer is essential for restoration. Christians worldwide must pray for God to call and equip more Christians to be missionaries on the world's mission fields. We pray to the Lord for restoration, justice, and peace for all peoples of the world. We pray that Christians everywhere will pray for God to restore world order. The time Christians devote to prayer determines how important restoring world order is on our priority lists. Praying daily for these concerns records our roles in restoring world order.

PRAYER: God of hosts, forgive us for the sins that we have committed against you, others, and the earth. Turn us from the path of destruction to the cross. Help us to govern ourselves according to your teachings. Make us wise in all things through Jesus Christ our Lord. Amen.

(LPT)

October 1

PRAYER CONCERN: **World hunger**
Blessed are you who hunger now, for you will be satisfied (Luke 6:21, NIV).

October 2

PRAYER CONCERN: **Persons displaced from their homeland**
The eternal God is thy refuge, and underneath are the everlasting arms (Deut. 33:27, KJV).

PRAYER CONCERN: War-torn countries

He makes wars cease to the ends of the earth;
he breaks the bow and shatters the spear
(Psalm 46:9, NIV).

October

3

**PRAYER CONCERN: Missionaries around
the world**

Jesus said, "Go ye therefore, and teach all
nations, baptizing them in the name of the
Father, and of the Son, and of the Holy Ghost"
(Matt. 28:19, KJV).

October

4

October

5

PRAYER CONCERN: **Foreign-service workers**

At this, [Ruth] bowed down with her face to the ground. She exclaimed, "Why have I found such favor in your eyes that you notice me— a foreigner?" (Ruth 2:10, NIV)

October

6

PRAYER CONCERN: **Worldwide leaders of the church**

Obey them that have the rule over you, and submit yourselves: for they watch for your souls, as they that must give an account, that they may do it with joy, and not with grief: for that is unprofitable for you (Heb. 13:17, KJV).

PRAYER CONCERN: World peace

Glory to God in the highest, and on earth peace to men on whom his favor rests (Luke 2:14, NIV).

October
7

I stopped mailing "Christmas cards" several years ago, I do mail a message—one that has nothing to do with Santa Claus or presents, but one that begs for prayers and for a world of peace and goodwill.

— Adam Clayton Powell

PRAYER CONCERN: Disarmament

And he shall judge among the nations and shall rebuke many people: and they shall beat their swords into plowshares, and their spears into pruning hooks: nation shall not lift up sword against nation, neither shall they learn war any more (Isa. 2:4, KJV).

October
8

October 9

PRAYER CONCERN: World trade

For everything created by God is good, and nothing is to be rejected, provided it is received with thanksgiving (1 Tim. 4:4, NRSV).

October 10

PRAYER CONCERN: A world free from terrorism

Jesus said, "I have told you these things, so that in me you may have peace. In this world you will have trouble. But take heart! I have overcome the world" (John 16:33, NIV).

PRAYER CONCERN: Workers who are underpaid

Do not rob or take advantage of anyone. Do not hold back the wages of someone you have hired, not even for one night (Lev. 19:13, TEV).

October
11

PRAYER CONCERN: World order

Of the increase of [Jesus'] government and peace there shall be no end, upon the throne of David, and upon his kingdom, to order it, and to establish it with judgment and with justice from henceforth even for ever. The zeal of the Lord of hosts will perform this (Isa. 9:7 KJV).

October
12

October

13

PRAYER CONCERN: **For Christian unity in developing countries**

Make every effort to keep the unity of the Spirit through the bond of peace (Eph. 4:3, NIV).

We must pray unrelentingly for economic justice, but we must also work diligently to bring into being those social changes that make for a better distribution of wealth within our nation and in the undeveloped countries of the world.

— Martin Luther King, Jr.

October

14

PRAYER CONCERN: **Economic power in developing countries**

In that day Israel will be one of three with Egypt and Assyria, even a blessing in the midst of the land (Isa. 19:24, NKJV).

PRAYER CONCERN: Foreign aid

The earth is the Lord's and all that is in it, the world, and those who live in it (Psalm 24:1, NRSV).

October
15

PRAYER CONCERN: For world public-health services

So [the good Samaritan] went to him and bandaged his wounds, pouring on oil and wine; and he set him on his own animal, brought him to an inn, and took care of him (Luke 10:34, NKJV).

October
16

October 17

PRAYER CONCERN: **World evangelism**
I will take you as My people, and I will be your God (Exod. 6:7, NKJV).

October 18

PRAYER CONCERN: **Countries that are experiencing drought**
Be glad then, you children of Zion, and rejoice in the Lord your God; for He has given you the former rain faithfully, and He will cause the rain to come down for you (Joel 2:23, NKJV).

PRAYER CONCERN: Poverty in the world

For the poor will never cease from the land; therefore I command you, saying, "You shall open your hand wide to your brother, to your poor and your needy, in your land" (Deut. 15:11, NKJV).

October

19

PRAYER CONCERN: Mother Africa

But you are a chosen race, a royal priesthood, a holy nation, God's own people, in order that you may proclaim the mighty acts of him who called you out of darkness into his marvelous light (1 Peter 2:9, NRSV).

October

20

October 21

PRAYER CONCERN: Social injustice

Speak and act as those who are going to be judged by the law that gives freedom, because judgment without mercy will be shown to anyone who has not been merciful. Mercy triumphs over judgment! (James 2:12-13, NIV)

Several generations of blacks suffered constant insults and abuses that were intended *to destroy pride and self-respect, but they prayed their way through it all. . . . We cannot accept injustices inflicted on others, and we will not participate in the infliction of such injustices ourselves.*

— Samuel D. Proctor

October 22

PRAYER CONCERN: Those who work in Christian world communications

How beautiful upon the mountains are the feet of him that bringeth good tidings, that publisheth peace; that bringeth good tidings of good, that publisheth salvation; that saith unto Zion, Thy God reigneth! (Isa. 52:7, KJV)

PRAYER CONCERN: Nonviolent social change

Violence shall no more be heard in your land, devastation or destruction within your borders; you shall call your walls Salvation and your gates Praise (Isa. 60:18, NRSV).

October
23

PRAYER CONCERN: Prisoners of war

Give ear to my words, O Lord, consider my meditation. Harken unto the voice of my cry, my King, and my God: for unto thee will I pray. My voice shalt thou hear in the morning, O Lord; in the morning will I direct my prayer unto thee, and will look up (Psalm 5:1-3, KJV).

October
24

October 25

PRAYER CONCERN: Rebuilding churches destroyed by war

Then all the people shouted with a great shout, when they praised the Lord, because the foundation of the house of the Lord was laid (Ezra 3:11*b*, NKJV).

October 26

PRAYER CONCERN: Human rights

Bear ye one another's burdens, and so fulfill the law of Christ (Gal. 6:2, KJV).

PRAYER CONCERN: World prayer

If my people, which are called by my name, shall humble themselves, and pray, and seek my face, and turn from their wicked ways; then will I hear from heaven, and will forgive their sin, and will heal their land (2 Chron. 7:14, KJV).

October
27

I find prayer is a two-way communication. Sometimes I find myself praying, "God, I cannot pray. Give me the words I need." God provides and keeps the communication open.

— Charlotte A. Meade

PRAYER CONCERN: Those who work in international affairs

For we are God's fellow workers; you are God's field, God's building (1 Cor. 3:9, NIV).

October
28

October 29

PRAYER CONCERN: **The Christian church worldwide**

For as we have many members in one body, and all members have not the same office: So we, being many, are one body in Christ, and every one members one of another (Rom. 12:4-5, KJV).

October 30

PRAYER CONCERN: **Developing countries**

Now it shall come to pass, if you diligently obey the voice of the Lord your God, to observe carefully all His commandments which I command you today, that the Lord your God will set you high above all nations of the earth (Deut. 28:1, NKJV).

PRAYER CONCERN: African unity

Let us therefore make every effort to do
what leads to peace and to mutual edification
(Rom. 14:19, NIV).

October
31

RISE AN' SHINE

Oh, rise an' shine an' give God de glory, glory,
Rise an' shine, an' give God de glory, glory,
Rise an' shine, an' give God de glory, glory,
For de year ob Juberlee.

Jesus carry de young lambs in his bosom, bosom,
Carry de young lambs in his bosom, bosom,
Carry de young lambs in his bosom, bosom
For de year ob Juberlee.

Jesus lead de ole sheep by still waters, waters,
Lead de ole sheep by still waters, waters,
Lead de ole sheep by still waters, waters,
For de year ob Juberlee.

NOVEMBER

PRAYERS
OF
THANKSGIVING

Offering Gratitude for the Good Shepherd

Today I write these lines with a heart overflowing with thankfulness to my Heavenly Father for His wonderful love & kindness; for His bountiful goodness to me, in that He has not caused me to want.

—IDA B. WELLS

ALTHOUGH DAVID WAS a shepherd, he too needed the protection of a caretaker. He expressed that care in the often-quoted Psalm 23. This psalm details the provisions of our Lord. God provides:

- the shelter of being our Shepherd (verse 1);
- rest, restoration, guidance, and righteous paths (verses 2–3);
- protection and comfort during troubled times (verse 4);
- blessings even in the midst of our enemies (verse 5);
- the anointing (verse 5);
- goodness and mercy (verse 6);
- a sacred dwelling place (verse 6).

As we read of God's provisions in Psalm 23, we, like Ida B. Wells, have reasons in abundance to be thankful. The Good Shepherd knows us and attentively meets all our needs. Jesus declares, "I am the good shepherd; I know my sheep and my sheep know me" (John 10:14, NIV). Sister Wells recognized that truth. Although she experienced tremendous hardships and pain—born a slave, orphaned at sixteen, raised five younger siblings, and endured deep isolation and loneliness—her journal recorded gratitude for a God who did not leave her destitute.

Remember, our God is changeless. As God was with David and with Ida B. Wells, God will be with us. The Good Shepherd protects and provides.

PRAYER: We praise you, our Good Shepherd, for your provisions. In you, O Lord, we have everything we need. Amen.

(KFW)

November 1

PRAYER OF THANKSGIVING: **For creating you**

I will praise thee; for I am fearfully and
wonderfully made: marvellous are thy works;
and that my soul knoweth right well
(Psalm 139:14, KJV).

November 2

PRAYER OF THANKSGIVING: **For God's mercy**

Thy mercy, O Lord, is in the heavens; and
thy faithfulness reacheth unto the clouds
(Psalm 36:5, KJV).

PRAYER OF THANKSGIVING: For God's greatness
I will proclaim the name of the Lord. Oh, praise
the greatness of our God! (Deut. 32:3, NIV)

November
3

PRAYER OF THANKSGIVING: For God's wisdom
O Lord, how manifold are thy works! in wisdom
hast thou made them all: the earth is full of thy
riches (Psalm 104:24, KJV).

November
4

November 5

PRAYER OF THANKSGIVING: For salvation

For God has destined us not for wrath but for obtaining salvation through our Lord Jesus Christ (1 Thess. 5:9, NRSV).

November 6

PRAYER OF THANKSGIVING: For God's holiness

Rejoice in the Lord, ye righteous; and give thanks at the remembrance of his holiness (Psalm 97:12, KJV).

PRAYER OF THANKSGIVING: For God's love

And we have known and believed the love that God hath to us. God is love; and he that dwelleth in love dwelleth in God, and God in him (1 John 4:16, KJV).

Heavenly Father, thank you for the spirit of love. May our lives demonstrate that your love is in us as we practice love toward others.

— Lloyd Preston Terrell

PRAYER OF THANKSGIVING: For peace

Let the peace of God rule in your hearts, since as members of one body you were called to peace (Col. 3:15, NIV).

PRAYER OF THANKSGIVING: For the air you breathe

For by him all things were created: things in heaven and on earth, visible and invisible, whether thrones or powers or rulers or authorities; all things were created by him and for him (Col. 1:16, NIV).

PRAYER OF THANKSGIVING: For a bill that you paid recently

And now, our God, we give thanks to you and praise your glorious name (1 Chron. 29:13, NRSV).

PRAYER OF THANKSGIVING: For healing you when you were sick

King Jeroboam said to the prophet, "Please pray for me to the Lord your God, and ask him to heal my arm!" The prophet prayed to the Lord, and the king's arm was healed (1 Kings 13:6, TEV).

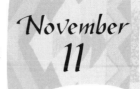

November
11

PRAYER OF THANKSGIVING: For providing guidance

For this God is our God for ever and ever: he will be our guide even unto death (Psalm 48:14, KJV).

November
12

November 13

PRAYER OF THANKSGIVING: For creation
The heavens declare the glory of God;
and the firmament sheweth his handiwork
(Psalm 19:1, KJV).

*It makes no difference
what one does or
what the situation
is, "A little talk wid
Jesus makes it right."
Complete reliance on
God is clearly seen
in the belief that
God answers prayers
and rewards those
who pray.*
— Benjamin E.
Mays

November 14

PRAYER OF THANKSGIVING: For answered prayer
Then shall ye call upon me, and ye shall go
and pray unto me, and I will hearken unto you
(Jer. 29:12, KJV).

PRAYER OF THANKSGIVING: For someone who is a new Christian

I tell you, there will be more joy in heaven over one sinner who repents than over ninety-nine righteous persons who need no repentance (Luke 15:7, NRSV).

November 15

PRAYER OF THANKSGIVING: For a person who gave you wise counsel

Listen to counsel and receive instruction, that you may be wise in your latter days (Prov. 19:20, NKJV).

November 16

November 17

PRAYER OF THANKSGIVING: **For heaven**

But our citizenship is in heaven. And we eagerly await a Savior from there, the Lord Jesus Christ, who, by the power that enables him to bring everything under his control, will transform our lowly bodies so that they will be like his glorious body (Phil. 3:20-21, NIV).

November 18

PRAYER OF THANKSGIVING: **For angels watching over you**

Are not all angels ministering spirits sent to serve those who will inherit salvation? (Heb. 1:14, NIV)

PRAYER OF THANKSGIVING: For your birthday

Come, let us bow down in worship, let us kneel before the Lord our Maker (Psalm 95:6, NIV).

November
19

PRAYER OF THANKSGIVING: For laughter

A merry heart doeth good like a medicine: but a broken spirit drieth the bones (Prov. 17:22, KJV).

November
20

November 21

PRAYER OF THANKSGIVING: **For a good friend**
A friend loves at all times (Prov. 17:17, NIV).

Thank God for the friends God sends to each of us. . . . friends who give more than they take, friends who bond with you on inarticulable levels. Friends who, when and if they must depart, leave you a better person than you were when they met you.

— Renita J. Weems

November 22

PRAYER OF THANKSGIVING: **For the Bible**
Thy word is a lamp unto my feet, and a light unto my path (Psalm 119:105, KJV).

PRAYER OF THANKSGIVING: For new beginnings

So if anyone is in Christ, there is a new creation: everything old has passed away; see, everything has become new! (2 Cor. 5:17, NRSV)

November

23

PRAYER OF THANKSGIVING: For your family

O Lord, you are my God; I will exalt you, I will praise your name; for you have done wonderful things (Isa. 25:1, NRSV).

November

24

November 25

PRAYER OF THANKSGIVING: **For rest**

Be at rest once more, O my soul, for the Lord has been good to you (Psalm 116:7, NIV).

November 26

PRAYER OF THANKSGIVING: **For the rain**

Sing to the Lord with thanksgiving; make music to our God on the harp. He covers the sky with clouds; he supplies the earth with rain and makes grass grow on the hills (Psalm 147:7-8, NIV).

PRAYER OF THANKSGIVING: For delivering you from a difficult situation

Then Moses and the Israelites sang this song to the Lord: "I will sing to the Lord, because he has won a glorious victory; he has thrown the horses and their riders into the sea. The Lord is my strong defender; he is the one who has saved me" (Exod. 15:1-2, TEV).

November 27

It is very good to wait in the presence of God and watch the concern of our private lives and our collective experiences take shape before our view. Our hearts are filled with praise and thanksgiving because we made it. We were not sure a week ago that we would.

— Howard Thurman

PRAYER OF THANKSGIVING: For allowing you to see another day

This is the day which the Lord hath made; we will rejoice and be glad in it (Psalm 118:24, KJV).

November 28

November 29

PRAYER OF THANKSGIVING: For your gifts and talents

There are different kinds of spiritual gifts, but the same Spirit gives them. There are different ways of serving, but the same Lord is served. . . . The Spirit's presence is shown in some way in each person for the good of all (1 Cor. 12:4-5, 7, TEV).

November 30

PRAYER OF THANKSGIVING: Thank God with your whole heart

I will praise thee, O Lord my God, with all my heart: and I will glorify thy name for evermore (Psalm 86:12, KJV).

DIDN'T MY LORD DELIVER DANIEL?

Chorus:
Didn't my Lord deliver Daniel,
D'liver Daniel, d'liver Daniel?
Didn't my Lord deliver Daniel,
And why not-a every man?

He deliver'd Daniel from the lion's den,
Jonah from the belly of the whale,
And the Hebrew children from the fiery furnace,
And why not-a every man?

The moon run down in a purple stream,
The sun forbear to shine,
And every star disappear,
King Jesus shall be mine.

The wind blows east, and the wind blows west,
It blows like the judgment day,
And every poor soul that never did pray,
'll be glad to pray that day.

I set my foot on the Gospel ship,
And the ship it began to sail,
It landed me over on Canaan's shore,
And I'll never come back anymore.

DECEMBER

PRAYERS
OF
HEALING
AND
DELIVERANCE

Trusting a God Who Delivers

It is important for the Church of God to tell the people of God, "Hey, hey, hey! Our God sees. Our God hears. Our God knows and our God will come down and deliver us."
— Desmond Tutu

A THIRTEEN-MONTH-OLD child was struggling for life, battling intestinal flu and dehydration. The prognosis was bad. "I do not think this child will live long enough for you to make it to the hospital," the family doctor told the parents. Still, he urged them to rush her immediately to Saint Augustine's Hospital in Raleigh, North Carolina.

In the hospital room, despair filled the parents' hearts as the silhouette of death hovered over their baby girl. When the mother left the child's room, she noticed a string that floated downward from the ceiling and she caught it. As she caught the string, the mother heard God say, "She is hanging between life and death."

When the parents returned home, the mother was so despondent that she could not bear to look at her infirmed child's clothes or toys. But that mother prayed. And as she prayed God not only affirmed that her child would be healed, but also that the mother needed to change her life and prepare for ministry. "Yes, Lord, whatever you have for me to do, I'll do it," she said.

That mother has been an ordained minister for more than thirty-five years. As for her once languishing child, she lived to write this meditation.

God is competent to handle your most difficult

problems. Psalm 34:15 confirms, "The eyes of the Lord are on the righteous and his ears are attentive to their cry" (NIV). Even when it seems that you are hanging in the balance of life and death, your God sees. Even when circumstances suggest that you are abandoned and your prayers unheard, your God hears (Psalm 34:17). Even when you feel misunderstood, your God knows (Psalm 34:22).

Proclaim words of hope, therefore, to your sisters and brothers when you see them in despair. A hope that declares, "Hey, hey, hey! . . . Our God will deliver us."

PRAYER: O God, our Healer and Deliverer, grant us faith in the midst of our hopelessness. Help us to remember that nothing is too difficult for you.

(KFW)

PRAYER CONCERN: Persons lured into cult activities

I urge you, brothers and sisters, to keep an eye on those who cause dissensions and offenses, in opposition to the teaching that you have learned; avoid them. For such people do not serve our Lord Christ, but their own appetites, and by smooth talk and flattery they deceive the hearts of the simple-minded (Rom. 16:17-18, NRSV).

PRAYER CONCERN: Persons who are suicidal

The Lord upholds all who are falling,
and raises up all who are bowed down
(Psalm 145:14, NRSV).

PRAYER CONCERN: Backsliders

I will heal their backsliding, I will love them freely (Hos. 14:4*a-b*, KJV).

December
3

PRAYER CONCERN: Persons who have been hurt by the church

The Lord is near to the brokenhearted, and saves the crushed in spirit (Psalm 34:18, NRSV).

December
4

PRAYER CONCERN: Persons who feel forsaken by God

There shall not any man be able to stand before thee all the days of thy life: as I was with Moses, so I will be with thee: I with not fail thee, nor forsake thee (Josh. 1:5, KJV).

PRAYER CONCERN: Persons suffering with insomnia

When you lie down, you will not be afraid; when you lie down, your sleep will be sweet (Prov. 3:24, NIV).

PRAYER CONCERN: Persons seeking an understanding of salvation

December 7

The eunuch asked Philip, "Tell me, please, who is the prophet talking about, himself or someone else?" Then Philip began with that very passage of Scripture and told him the good news about Jesus (Acts 8:34-35, NIV).

*Dear Jesus unto Thee
  we cry,
Give us the
  preparation;
Turn not away thy
  tender eye;
We seek thy true
  salvation.*

— Jupiter Hammon

PRAYER CONCERN: Persons consumed with Christmas commercialism

December 8

And the world and its desire are passing away, but those who do the will of God live forever (1 John 2:17, NRSV).

December 9

PRAYER CONCERN: Persons with sexual addictions

Flee from sexual immorality. . . . Do you not know that your body is a temple of the Holy Spirit, who is in you, whom you have received from God? You are not your own; you were bought at a price. Therefore honor God with your body (1 Cor. 6:18*a*, 19-20, NIV).

December 10

PRAYER CONCERN: Persons unable to forgive themselves

My dear children, I write this to you so that you will not sin. But if anybody does sin, we have one who speaks to the Father in our defense— Jesus Christ, the Righteous One. He is the atoning sacrifice for our sins, and not only for ours but also for the sins of the whole world (1 John 2:1, NIV).

PRAYER CONCERN: Persons who need courage

Be of good courage, and he shall strengthen
your heart, all ye that hope in the Lord
(Psalm 31:24, KJV).

December
11

PRAYER CONCERN: Persons filled with pride

When pride comes, then comes disgrace, but
with humility comes wisdom (Prov. 11:2, NIV).

December
12

December 13

PRAYER CONCERN: Persons who are insecure

Paul said, "Such confidence as this is ours through Christ before God. Not that we are competent to claim anything for ourselves, but our competence comes from God" (2 Cor. 3:4-5, NIV).

If we can find time for being quiet and still during this holiday season—and throughout the coming year—we will hear God speak quietly but earnestly to our souls.

—Alfred L. Norris

December 14

PRAYER CONCERN: Persons asking God for direction

Show me your ways, O Lord, teach me your paths; guide me in your truth and teach me, for you are God my Savior, and my hope is in you all day long (Psalm 25:4-5, NIV).

PRAYER CONCERN: Persons confused about their salvation

God is not the author of confusion, but of peace (1 Cor. 14:33*a*, KJV).

PRAYER CONCERN: Persons who need a new start

Remember ye not the former things, neither consider the things of old. Behold, I will do a new thing; now it shall spring forth; shall ye not know it? I will even make a way in the wilderness, and rivers in the desert (Isa. 43:18-19, KJV).

December 17

PRAYER CONCERN: **Safety for persons with hazardous or dangerous professions**

You are a hiding place for me; you preserve me from trouble; you surround me with glad cries of deliverance (Psalm 32:7, NRSV).

December 18

PRAYER CONCERN: **Persons who manage time poorly**

Jesus said, "We must work the works of him who sent me while it is day; night is coming when no one can work" (John 9:4, NRSV).

PRAYER CONCERN: Complacent Christians
But the end of all things is at hand:
be ye therefore sober, and watch unto prayer
(1 Peter 4:7, KJV).

December
19

**PRAYER CONCERN: Persons who need help
controlling their temper**
You must understand this, my beloved: let
everyone be quick to listen, slow to speak, slow
to anger; for your anger does not produce
God's righteousness (James 1:19-20, NRSV).

December
20

December 21

PRAYER CONCERN: Persons who are brokenhearted

He healeth the broken in heart, and bindeth up their wounds (Psalm 147:3, KJV).

If a promise is not kept . . . or if I experience long-lasting pain, I begin to doubt God and God's love. I fall so miserably into the chasm of disbelief that I cry out in despair. . . . when I cry out earnestly I am answered immediately and am returned to faithfulness.

— Maya Angelou

December 22

PRAYER CONCERN: Persons harboring unforgiveness

Then came Peter to him, and said, Lord, how oft shall my brother sin against me, and I forgive him? till seven times? Jesus saith unto him, I say not unto thee, Until seven times: but, Until seventy times seven (Matt. 18:21-22, KJV).

PRAYER CONCERN: Persons suffering holiday depression

The righteous cry, and the Lord heareth, and delivereth them out of all their troubles (Psalm 34:17, KJV).

PRAYER CONCERN: Persons alone during the holiday

For the mountains may depart and the hills may be removed, but my steadfast love shall not depart from you, and my covenant of peace shall not be removed, says the Lord, who has compassion on you (Isa. 54:10, NRSV).

December 25

PRAYER CONCERN: Praise God for Jesus the Savior

And the angel said unto them, Fear not: for, behold, I bring you good tidings of great joy, which shall be to all people. For unto you is born this day in the city of David a Saviour, which is Christ the Lord (Luke 2:10-11, KJV).

December 26

PRAYER CONCERN: Persons blinded to their own faults

Teach me, O Lord, to follow your decrees; then I will keep them to the end. . . . Turn my heart toward your statutes and not toward selfish gain (Psalm 119:33, 36, NIV).

PRAYER CONCERN: Persons bound by fear

The Lord is my light and my salvation; whom shall I fear? the Lord is the strength of my life; of whom shall I be afraid?
(Psalm 27:1, KJV)

December
27

If you know how to stay in touch with God, you can win any battle.

— A minister, name unknown

PRAYER CONCERN: Persons in support groups

The Lord your God is with you; his power gives you victory. The Lord will take delight in you, and in his love he will give you new life
(Zeph. 3:17, TEV).

December
28

December 29

PRAYER CONCERN: Persons who are workaholics

It is vain that you rise up early and go late to rest, eating the bread of anxious toil; for [the Lord] gives sleep to his beloved (Psalm 127:2, NRSV).

December 30

PRAYER CONCERN: Persons who gossip

Let no corrupt communication proceed out of your mouth, but that which is good to the use of edifying, that it may minister grace unto the hearers (Eph. 4:29, KJV).

PRAYER CONCERN: Someone you find difficult to love

December 31

Love your enemies and pray for those who persecute you, so that you may be children of your Father in heaven. . . . For if you love those who love you, what reward do you have? (Matt. 5:44-45*a*, 46, NRSV)

PREFACE

Melva Wilson Costen, *African American Christian Worship* (Nashville: Abingdon Press, 1993), 106.

JANUARY

Marjorie L. Kimbrough, *Beyond Limitation: Encouragement and Inspiration for the Start of Your Career* (Nashville: Abingdon Press, 1993), 117.

Wyatt Tee Walker, *Spirits That Dwell in Deep Woods III: The Prayer and Praise Hymns of the Black Religious Experience* (New York: Martin Luther King Fellows Press, 1991), 59.

Woodie W. White, *Confessions of a Prairie Pilgrim* (Nashville: Abingdon Press, 1988), 29.

Augustine of Hippo: Selected Writings, trans. Mary T. Clark (New York: Paulist Press, 1984), 122.

FEBRUARY

A. Clayton Powell, Sr., *Against the Tide: An Autobiography* (New York: Richard R. Smith, 1938), 165.

Sheron C. Patterson, *I Want To Be Ready: Meditations Based on Quotes from Famous Black Persons* (Nashville: Abingdon Press, 1994), 44.

Richard Allen, *The Life Experience and Gospel Labors of the Rt. Rev. Richard Allen* (Nashville: Abingdon Press, 1960), 43.

Preston Robert Washington, *God's Transforming Spirit: Black Church Renewal* (Valley Forge, Pa.: Judson Press, 1988), 48.

Charles T. Walker, *Life of Charles T. Walker, D.D.* (New York: Negro Universities Press, 1902; 1969), 131.

MARCH

John Perkins, *With Justice for All* (Ventura, Calif.: Regal Books, 1982), 192.

Georgia Montgomery Davis Powers in Brian Lanker, *I Dream A World: Portraits of Black Women Who Changed America* (New York: Stewart, Tabori & Chang, 1989), 71.

Roosevelt Darby Jr. in William J. Key and Robert Johnson-Smith II, eds., *From One Brother to Another: Voices of African-American Men* (Valley Forge, Pa.: Judson Press, 1996), 59.

Eugene F. Rivers 3d, "Blocking the Prayers of the Church," *Sojourners* (March/April 1997), 29.

Anthony T. Evans, *America's Only Hope: Impacting Society in the 90s* (Chicago: Moody Press, 1990), 167.

APRIL

Edward P. Wimberly, *Prayer in Pastoral Counseling: Suffering, Healing, and Discernment* (Louisville, Ky.: Westminster/John Knox Press, 1990), 11.

Roderick Rogers, a native of North Carolina, received a heart transplant in 1994.

Onnie Lee Logan, as told to Katherine Clark; *Motherwit: An Alabama Midwife's Story* (New York: E. P. Dutton, 1989), 144.

Orleans Finger in B. A. Botkin, ed., *Lay My Burden Down: A Folk History of Slavery* (Chicago: University of Chicago Press, 1945), 34.

MAY

John Biggers in *Black Art Ancestral Legacy: The African Impulse in African-American Art* (New York: Dallas Museum of Art and Harry N. Abrams, Inc., 1989), 118.

Kenneth L. Waters Sr., *I Saw the Lord: A Pilgrimage Through Isaiah 6* (Nashville: Upper Room Books, 1996), 30.

Marjorie L. Kimbrough, *She Is Worthy: Encounters with Biblical Women* (Nashville: Abingdon Press, 1994), 122–123.

JUNE

T. D. Jakes, *Loose That Man & Let Him Go!* (Tulsa: Albury Publishing, 1995), 158–159.

Jakes, *Loose That Man & Let Him Go!*, 160.

Gardner C. Taylor, *Chariots Aflame* (Nashville: Broadman Press, 1988), 49.

Crawford W. Loritts, *A Passionate Commitment* (San Bernardino, Calif.: Here's Life Publishers, Inc., 1989), 59–60.

Jawanza Kunjufu, *Adam! Where Are You? Why Most Black Men Don't Go to Church* (Chicago: African American Images, 1994), iii.

JULY

James Forbes, Jr. in Marian Wright Edelman, *Guide My Feet* (Boston: Beacon Press, 1995), 43.

Marian Wright Edelman, "A Conversation with Marian Wright Edelman," *Alive Now* (July/August 1997), 43.

Holding Children in Prayer: A Lenten Guide (Washington, D.C.: The Children's Defense Fund, 1997), 39.

Daniel H. Peterson, *The Looking-Glass: Being a True Report and Narrative of the Life, Travels, and Labors of the Rev. Daniel H. Peterson* (New York: Wright, Printer, 1854), 14, 17.

Patricia and Fredrick McKissack, *When Do You Talk to God? Prayers for Small Children* (Minneapolis: Augsburg Publishing House, 1986), 19.

AUGUST

John Wesley Work, *Folk Song of the American Negro* (Nashville: Press of Fisk University, 1915), 80.

Lloyd Preston Terrell, *Pray, Pastor, Pray!* (Columbus, Ga.: Brentwood Christian Press, 1993), 22.

Rosa Parks with Gregory J. Reed, *Quiet Strength: The Faith, the Hope, and the Heart of a Woman Who Changed a Nation* (Grand Rapids, Mich.: Zondervan, 1994), 54.

Kevin W. Cosby in J. Alfred Smith Sr., ed., *No Other Help I Know: Sermons on Prayer and Spirituality* (Valley Forge, Pa.: Judson Press, 1996), 29.

Sarah and A. Elizabeth Delany with Amy Hill Hearth, *The Delany Sisters' Book of Everyday Wisdom* (New York: Kodansha, 1994), 52.

SEPTEMBER

Rackham Holt, *George Washington Carver: An American Biography* (Garden City, N.Y.: Doubleday & Company, 1943, 1963), 232–233.

Ella Pearson Mitchell in J. Alfred Smith Sr., ed., *No Other Help I Know: Sermons on Prayer and Spirituality* (Valley Forge, Pa.: Judson Press, 1996), 46.

Terrell, *Pray, Pastor, Pray!*, 56.

Sojourner Truth, *Narrative of Sojourner Truth*, ed. Margaret Washington (New York: Vintage Classics, 1993), 53.

Robert E. Dungy, *Dimensions in Black Spirituality* (Nashville: Upper Room Books, 1991), 49.

OCTOBER

Bernice A. King, *Hard Questions, Heart Answers: Speeches and Sermons* (New York: Broadway Books, 1996), 49.

Adam Clayton Powell, *Keep the Faith, Baby!* (New York: Trident Press, 1967), 101.

Martin Luther King, Jr., *Strength to Love* (Philadelphia: Fortress Press, 1963), 132.

Samuel D. Proctor and Willam D. Watley, eds., *Sermons from the Black Pulpit* (Valley Forge, Pa.: Judson Press, 1984), 30.

Charlotte A. Meade in O. Richard Bowyer, Betty Hart, and Charlotte A. Meade, *Prayer in the Black Tradition* (Nashville: The Upper Room, 1986), 107.

NOVEMBER

Ida B. Wells, *The Memphis Diary of Ida B. Wells*, ed. Miriam DeCosta-Willis (Boston: Beacon Press, 1995), 150–151.

Terrell, *Pray, Pastor, Pray!*, 72.

Benjamin E. Mays, *The Negro's God as Reflected in His Literature* (Boston: Chapman & Grimes, Inc., 1938), 21.

Renita J. Weems, "Missing Jonathan," *The Other Side* (January/February 1997), 54.

Howard Thurman, *The Centering Moment* (Richmond, Ind.: Friends United Press, 1969), 76.

DECEMBER

Desmond Tutu, *The Rainbow People of God*, ed. John Allen (New York: Doubleday, 1994), 164.

Jupiter Hammon in J. Saunders Redding, *To Make a Poet Black* (Chapel Hill: The University of North Carolina Press, 1939), 5.

Alfred L. Norris, "God's Silent Gift Speaks Volumes," *The Interpreter* (November/December 1995), 13.

Maya Angelou, *Wouldn't Take Nothing for My Journey Now* (New York: Random House, 1993), 34–35.

Benjamin Elijah Mays and Joseph William Nicholson, *The Negro's Church* (New York: Institute of Social and Religious Research, 1933), 87. Mays studied the content of 100 sermons that he and Nicholson collected between 1930–1931. The quotation on December 27 is an excerpt from one of these sermons. The minister is not known.

The Authors

I was nurtured in a home where family prayer, faith in God, and prayer meetings were taught and experienced. These early sacred memories not only inspired me to develop a personal relationship with God, but also encouraged me to integrate prayer into every aspect of my life. The assurance that I can talk to God about anything, at any place, and at any time is an awesome privilege that I can compare to none other.

KAREN F. WILLIAMS is an associate editor of Upper Room Books in Nashville, Tennessee. Prior to this position she was a Sunday school curriculum editor and writer for The United Methodist Publishing House. A native of Raleigh, North Carolina, she received a B.A. degree in English from North Carolina Agricultural and Technical State University and a M.A. in Communication from Regent University (formerly CBN University). She enjoys playwriting, reading, and photography.

Prayer has released power in my life to be an effective Christian husband, father, pastor, and community leader. Through prayer, I have learned to listen to God and take action to do the things that God has called me to do. My prayer journey started when I was a boy at Mount Zion Baptist Church in Akron, Ohio, where the saints encouraged me to find joy in praying.

LLOYD PRESTON TERRELL is the pastor of Franklin-Saint John's United Methodist Church in Newark, New Jersey, He also serves as Adjunct Professor of Supervised Ministry at Drew University and as Adjunct Professor at Zarepath Bible Institute. He holds degrees from Paine College (B.A.), the University of Dubuque (M.Div.) and New York Theological Seminary (D.Min.). He is also the author of *Pray, Pastor, Pray!* He and his wife, Marguerite, have four children: Lloyd Jr., Alice, Ralph, and Zelma. Dr. Terrell's hobbies include reading, writing, and collecting memorabilia on the African American pastor.